Startup

From Idea to Launch: Navigating the Four Stages of a Startup Business

MATTHEW SMITH
JESSICA DAWSON

maven

Copyright © 2016 by Matthew Smith and Jessica Dawson

Maven Publishing USA

First Edition

For information about special discounts for bulk purchases or author interviews and appearances please contact Maven Publishing USA at info@maven-books.com.

ISBN-10: 0-9970523-1-7

ISBN-13: 978-0-9970523-1-2

Who Is This Book For?

First of all, welcome! You picked this book up for a reason, and we're glad you did. Before we get too deep into the Four Stages of Starting a Business, we want to make sure you're going to get something useful from it. While we believe that there are nuggets of advice throughout this book that could apply to anyone, we did write this book with certain types of people in mind. If you're one of them, we hope you learn a lot as you read and put these ideas into practice. If you're not, we hope you find some helpful information in here, but we also realize that there are large portions of the book that won't be relevant to you.

As the title suggests, we wrote this book mainly to help people who are starting their own business for the first time. If you're thinking about becoming an entrepreneur, but need some guidance from people who have already done it, this book is a great place to begin. We go through the entire process of getting a business up and running from the moment you first have the idea, all the way through a successful launch, and we dissect the various things you need to think about during each stage of the process. We've each added our own perspectives throughout, and how these concepts have applied to our own respective ventures.

If you're not a first-time entrepreneur, there is plenty here for you. We have both learned by doing, and we've made mistakes that have helped us improve our companies. If you started a company that didn't do as well as you hoped, and you're trying again with a new business, hopefully you'll find some wisdom in this book that keeps you from repeating your previous mistakes. At the very least, we hope you'll be able to recognize the pitfalls from your past attempts, and you'll be reminded that mistakes are just part of the process.

Some of you may have actually been in business for a number of years, but are feeling like you're in startup mode again. Maybe your industry changed dramatically, and you have to learn how to stay competitive. Maybe you experienced a major downsizing, and you need to figure out how to operate on a smaller budget with a smaller team. Whatever the case may be, feeling like a brand new business owner again is uncomfortable and foreign. We hope the advice here helps you remember what it was like to be starting for the first time, and we hope you get some ideas for how to handle your new situation.

Who We Are and Why We Wrote This Book

Matt is a small business enthusiast and the CEO of Modmacro, a boutique digital marketing firm that's focused on growing businesses by targeting the correct audiences, and building brands by sharing their story.

Jessica is CEO and Co-founder of Maven Publishing, a small publishing house that works with small business owners, entrepreneurs, and professionals to create books that position them as experts in their fields and that become powerful marketing assets for their businesses.

We're both passionate about our own businesses, and we both love working with other small businesses and making sure they have the tools they need in order to be successful.

This is not meant to be a how-to book. Neither of us claims to be the absolute authority on starting a business. We've both done it successfully, but each of us has approached it a little differently, and we recognize there are very few things that are all good or all bad. We hope our advice and perspectives are useful, but we also understand that you need to do what makes sense to you and your business. Don't feel like you need to follow everything in a linear fashion. We've presented the Four Stages of Starting a Business in chronological order, but within those stages, each business and each situation will require a different approach.

We think it's exciting that you want to start a business. It's one of the most freeing and challenging experiences life has to offer. It's not for the faint-of-heart or anyone who fears making mistakes. As you start putting the concepts into action, you'll find out very quickly whether or not entrepreneurship is for you. We hope it is, and we hope you love it more and more the longer you're in business.

Best of luck,

Matt & Jessica

Stage One:
Ideation

Why Start a Business?

I F YOU'VE MADE it to this chapter, congratulations! That means you're reading the right book, and you're looking for some real advice from real business owners. You probably haven't gotten very far into making plans yet, and that's exactly why we believe this book will help you. In our experience, one of the best ways to avoid common pitfalls is to set yourself up for success right from the beginning by thinking about certain things ahead of time.

We know there's a reason you believe starting a business is the right path for you, and in this first section, we'll explore some of those reasons. No reasons for starting a business are "bad" or "wrong," but knowing why your business idea is so important to you can help you get off on the right foot.Choosing to start a business is a powerful decision. It brings with it a great sense of freedom, but also a great sense of responsibility. In other words, the plus side is that you'll be calling your own shots, but the downside. . . is that you'll be calling your own shots. For many people, that combination is what draws them in—the exhilaration and the challenge of making all the decisions.So let's go through some of the thoughts and ideas that inspire people to make the decision to go out on their own. Do you see yourself in any of these examples? Maybe your story fits one of them exactly, or maybe it's a combination of several. Whatever your reason, it's important to identify it, explore it, and remember it. When things get tough (because they most certainly will), that reason will be the shining light that keeps you going.

You Have a Passion for _____, and You Want to Make a Living From It

In a perfect world, we would all be passionate about the work we do. That's really the American Dream; you can pursue anything you want, and if you can find a way to make money out of something you enjoy, more power to you.

This is a great reason to start a business. As the saying goes, "find something you love, and you'll never work a day in your life." If you can get up each morning, do something that is fun and gratifying for you, *and* make enough money from it to live your life, you've got it made.

This comes up a lot with people who are hobbyists and who want to take their hobby to the next level. For example, someone who loves working on cars may dream of starting their own mechanic shop. Someone who loves working with computers may have a desire to start a repair shop or become an IT consultant of some kind. Crafters of handmade goods often dream of opening up their own shops and selling their goods either online or in a brick and mortar store.

Here's the thing to keep in mind: While you absolutely need a lot of passion for what you do in order to make a business out of it, you must also be aware that working directly on your primary product or service will only be a percentage of what you need to do as a business owner. And with time and success, that percentage decreases.

Not everyone thinks about this when they set out to start their business, and this is why some people end up either failing or giving up after a short while. They get excited about going full-time with their hobby, but then they lose some of that passion once they start getting into the nitty-gritty of business ownership.

We suggest looking into some of the administrative things it takes to run a business. How much of it are you interested in learning about? What can you delegate to a professional? Is there anything that you're intimidated by or that you worry about your ability to learn? Do your research so that you at least have a basic working knowledge of what you'll need to do to get your business off the ground and keep it running.

Hopefully, if you aren't already, you'll quickly become excited at the prospect of having your professional destiny in your hands. Each of those administrative tasks—accounting, maintenance, legal structure, sales, inventory, etc.—directly affects the future of your business and being the one to make those decisions can be fun and empowering. Remember, you're the one who gets to call all the shots now, and while you should rely on professionals for certain things (more on that in a later chapter), being the one in charge means you are the one who gets to take credit for your business's success!

✠ Matt: I've said for years that an estimated 75 percent of what you do as a business owner is stuff other than the product or service you provide. So if you love being an architect, that's great, but if you decide to start a company, you'd better also love invoicing, project management, paying bills, strategic business development, sales, etc. Once you find those tasks that you either can't do (for lack of knowledge, education, or licensing) or that you simply don't want to do, that will be your first list of professionals to contact and staff members to bring on.

As my company grows, I'm constantly surprised at how much time I end up investing in project management, client relationship management, operations, and strategic development.

✠ Jessica: Long before I became a publisher, I was managing my own career as a freelance writer. While I didn't have many complications to deal with because I was working by myself out of my home, I still had to learn to manage my business; I had to go out and get clients, and I had to keep track of my income. It wasn't hard, necessarily, but it took more time that I would have expected.

Now, as a publisher, our business model is about as simple as it can be. Still, there are things I have to do that have nothing to do with writing or publishing. There are weeks during which I feel like I'm just talking to my attorney and accountant instead of doing anything related to our books or authors.

There are days when I don't feel like I know what I'm doing with all that administrative stuff, but at the same time, I am energized and empowered by the fact that those decisions are mine and my partner's to make. We don't have to wait for a boss to tell us what to do.

Think about it: When you visualize your new life as a business owner, how do you see yourself handling the day-to-day operations, even when they don't seem related to your product or service? Does that part of it still sound fun to you? Even if it's not your favorite thing to think about, does it at least sound manageable?

As you get further into the process of starting your business, these are serious questions you need to ask yourself to determine whether business ownership is truly something you want.

You Saw Someone Doing _____ as a Business, and You Think You Can Do It Better

Many people have been in this scenario: You're at a restaurant or local shop, and something doesn't meet your expectations. You think, "If this were my business, I'd run it so much better." If you have that experience enough times, it can motivate you to want to start your own version of that business.

The same is true when you work for a company that is run poorly. Because you spend so much time in it, you can get a genuine feel for what goes on behind the scenes. Many people choose to start businesses of their own because they've had so much firsthand experience of what not to do, and they know they can do better.

That's the advantage to seeing someone else do something first. You can sit back, analyze their strengths and weaknesses, and take notes for yourself. You can work solutions for obvious problems into your own business plan, so that when you're ready to launch, you've already corrected something that was an issue for someone else.

By evaluating another business, either as a customer or as an employee, you're also critically thinking about your own business idea. You're solidifying your commitment to it, and you're increasing your chances that it will be successful.

At the same time, looking at someone else's business can be tricky. Some things will seem laughably obvious. Maybe the business is in a strange location; maybe their customer service department isn't very efficient; maybe their product could use a slight adjustment. The thing to remember is that the person making those decisions made them for a reason. Of course, they may be looking back on some of those decisions, thinking, "Wow, that was a big mistake," but they also may stand by those decisions, even if they don't seem ideal from the outside.

For example, there is a local brewery in northern California that does an extremely limited release of a particular beer each year. People line up on that day at the crack of dawn, and the line always goes around the block. They run out of the beer within hours. People often say things like, "They should just make an extra batch. They'd make more money!" Or even, "They should raise the price on it!" From an outside perspective, these seem like simple ways to improve the business's bottom line, but the business isn't broken. Does it really need fixing?

What they've done is perfect for them: They've created scarcity, so they can ensure that people will come out on that day to get something they may not otherwise be able to get. They've also found a price point that people are willing to line up for. If it were more expensive, people may not think waiting around is worth the cost, and they would be less likely to spend time in the shop, potentially buying additional products. If it were cheaper, people may not see enough value in that one beer to come out at all.

So by all means, observe, take notes, and learn from others' mistakes. At the same time, be careful about making assumptions, because a choice may have been made for a logical and business savvy reason. If you can, build relationships with other business owners so you can ask them questions about what they did and didn't do when starting their businesses. You may learn that what initially seems like a misstep may be an important choice to make in your own business.

✚ Matt: I had always wanted to build my own company, and I really wasn't doing well with working for people who were constantly making bad decisions. It was all big stuff, too, like missing paychecks, not looking at profitability, and people being emotional in their decision-making. Then the employees would later find out that a bookkeeper or manager had been embezzling huge amounts for years.

I'd been through that with a few companies, both big and small, so it had nothing to do with the size of the company. It had everything to do with the fact that a lot of people don't know how to run a business. And of course, some people can't be trusted. I never thought I'd be a great business leader per se; it just seemed like I'd seen enough examples of what not to do that I could learn from that and do it better. As it turns out, small business management, strategy, and marketing were untapped passions that I both enjoy and have some talents for.

On the topic of trying to run a company "better" than others, what I've found is that sometimes successfully positioning yourself isn't as much about being better as it is about being different. For example, at Modmacro, we approach web design projects in a much different way than most of our competitors. Most companies focus on the visual design and the implementation thereof. That means the client is left to work out everything else; writing the content, crafting the calls to action, gathering photography, deciding what pages are most important and how they are presented, etc. That also means that important technical and foundational elements are often overlooked.

Search Engine Optimization (SEO), for example, starts at the programming level. As a result, design-focused companies often completely miss the importance of developing with Google best practices in mind, or considering more advanced elements like structured data markup to improve search engine click through rates (CTRs). In contrast, we approach these projects in a holistic manner, and we have the expertise in-house to do everything from branding and copywriting to design, programming and SEO. Does that make us better? Maybe. But it certainly makes us different. Additionally, the ability to articulate differences can be key when presenting a value proposition.

╫ Jessica: I also had the frustrating experience of working for a business that wasn't run very well. They were in the industry I wanted to be in, but the way they were handling customers was not healthy for the business. Being able to experience those mistakes firsthand helped me understand what needed to be changed in my own company moving forward.

I've also had the opportunity to talk to owners of local businesses I like to frequent and ask them questions about some of the choices they've made. My favorite coffee shop is a great example. I've never run a coffee shop before, but as a customer, there are some things that I feel like I would change if the business were mine. After sitting down with the owner of my favorite shop, though, I'm not so sure. The decisions she's made are on-brand for her, and anything else wouldn't fit.

Observing someone else's business can be great research, whether or not they're successful, and sometimes you can learn more valuable lessons from a poorly-run business than from a well-run one. The thing to keep in mind is to understand the "whys" behind the actions so that you can make informed decisions for your own situation.

You Believe Starting Your Own Business Will Make You a Lot of Money

This probably seems obvious. Anyone who starts a business needs to think about making money. After all, a business will only remain in business if there is money in the bank to keep it going. When you are the one running the show, you have so much control over how your business's income is used, and if you're planning on going into business by yourself and for yourself, it seems like it could be a way to make a lot of money.

Money is a great reason to go into business, and wanting to become more autonomous with your finances is a great goal. Managing the financial aspects of a business, or hiring someone to do it for you, is thrilling, in a way. Where the goal of making money becomes problematic is when it's the only goal. If your sole motivation for wanting to start a business is so you can make a lot of money, you may find that you run into trouble.

No matter what you do, work is still work. Running a business is not easy, and there are going to be parts of the process that are not fun. There may even be times when your business is not making the kind of money you hoped for. To get through those times, and to keep your business going even when it's challenging, there has to be something substantial in it for you. If money is the only goal, and money is part of the challenge, then the temptation to quit when things get tough is very strong.

Another thing to consider is risk. When you're blinded by the excitement of starting a business that you're sure is going to make a lot of money, you're likely to gloss over the potential downsides, and you may forget to ask yourself some important questions:

- Are you the sole or primary breadwinner for your family?
- Will this business require a substantial initial investment?
- Do you need to spend time and/or money on education or certifications before you can start?

All of these questions can help you assess your initial risk. It's great to be confident as you're just starting to put your business plans together, but you have to also be realistic. If that great payday doesn't come right away, are you still going to be able to keep yourself and your family afloat in the meantime?Going into business with the goal of making money. It's a great goal; but make sure there is more to it so that you have something to get you through the tough times and so that you can start off with realistic expectations of what is at stake.

✝ Matt: It's important to consider the profitability, and therefore the sustainability of your potential business. The idea of making money is certainly core to the idea of becoming a business owner, but most aspiring business owners who think they've found a great way to make money tend to downplay the cost of operation. They have the sales figures all figured out, but they've grossly underestimated the costs associated with launching and running the business.

To start with, they often don't have a marketing budget, yet they call a company like mine to talk about marketing services. They are often enamored with the prospect of great revenues, but that blinds them to the reality of what business ownership is, what the costs are (both hard and soft), and the fact that business ownership can be a grind. I've found that most people can't stay motivated to grind it out if their sole motivation is money.

✝ Jessica: I'm not sure I would have had the guts to start a business if I'd only been thinking about money. I'm cautious by nature, probably more than I need to be, and the idea of making a "quick buck" just sounds foreign to me. Thankfully, I've met a lot of entrepreneurs who are much more hopeful and optimistic, which balances me out. I think to start a business and keep it going, you need to either be able to balance those two tendencies yourself, or you need to go into business with someone who sees this differently than you do. It keeps you out of trouble.

When I've seen people chasing money as the only objective for starting a business, the main thing I see is a lack of focus. There's a lot of jumping around. There's a lot of following fads, only to see them die months, sometimes weeks later. If there's no coherent vision that drives the desire to make money, it's hard to build a brand, and it's hard to create loyalty with customers. It can even be hard to find customers in the first place, because you're just chasing the next "big thing" without developing what you already have.

Money is such a tricky topic because you need to have it. You have to make money somehow, or your business won't survive. Yet, if left totally unchecked, money can end up being your business's downfall, even if you have plenty of it. It's a motivator, but it can be an empty one if there's no focus or passion behind the business in the first place.

Moving Forward with Your Idea

So you have your idea, and you've thought about the reasons why you want to go for it. You're ready to think about it more and take the next step toward making your business idea a reality, which means you're going to go through some phases of thought and planning. It's important to know what's ahead so that you can keep moving and not get stuck in any one phase. Each of these stagess is necessary, and each requires some time. Still, it's very easy to overthink it and stall yourself.

Ideas are Flowing Like Crazy

Those first moments when you decide you're going to make the leap and start a business are so exciting. You think of all the freedom and possibilities, and it is one of the best feelings out there. In those first waves of optimism, it's common to be flooded with ideas, and that's a good thing. You'll need some, if not all, of those ideas later. This stage is fun because it ramps up your energy. You're not thinking that everything could go wrong, and it allows you to gain confidence in what you're about to do. It will provide energy that will sustain you once you start implementing things and doing the actual hard work. Because this stage is so full of hope, you'll be open to creative ideas that you may not have thought of otherwise, and sometimes, those "aha" moments that come out of this stage end up being pivotal aspects of your eventual business.

That's the great news. Unfortunately, there's also a bit of a downside. All that energy can be shockingly unproductive if it's not controlled. When ideas are coming at you out of left field and when every idea seems like a good one, it's very easy to lose focus. Many wannabe small business owners get lost here. How do you know which ideas to follow and which ideas to leave by the wayside? How do you prevent yourself from going down a rabbit hole that will only distract you from getting your business started?Awareness is the key. If you're the kind of person who enjoys structure and discipline, you might find it helpful to actually schedule time for brainstorming and daydreaming about your future success. If you have a partner or other people you're working with, plan to have calls that are specifically for this purpose so that you don't end up wasting time.Some people have a tough time "planning for spontaneity," and that's understandable. It's perfectly fine to allow creativity to flow when the mood strikes; it's just imperative to be aware of the time spent so that you stay on top of more grounded tasks and don't lose focus. Remember that your goal is to get your business off the ground, and while allowing a bunch of ideas to flood in can be helpful to a point, too much brainstorming can be a distraction.

Another issue that comes into play during this stage is what we like to call "analysis paralysis." This happens when you come up with a whole bunch of good ideas, and then recognize that you have to choose only one. For example, choosing a company name can be both the most fun part and the most agonizing part of starting a business. In a single brainstorming session, you may come up with a dozen ideas for a name that are all good. The problem is that you can only pick one.

You've done the right thing by staying focused— after all, you've only been thinking about one thing: your company's name. Still, you've come up with a bunch of ideas, and you can't keep them all. There's no formula for choosing the perfect company name; much of that has to come from intuition. Narrow down your list by trusting your gut instinct, and then get feedback from others if you still can't pick one.

The key is not to spend too much time on it. Analysis paralysis will set in, and you won't be able to move on to the next important step. If you're really struggling and having trouble moving forward, you may benefit from reaching out to marketing or branding experts. Companies like Modmacro help startups create coherent branding, and a good, memorable company name is arguably the most important piece. Working with an expert will help you get out of your head and evaluate your options more objectively.

✚ Matt: Options can be a dangerous thing to have. Analysis paralysis is all too common. Most people can't process several choices all at the same time. Here's a simple technique to break all the options down into a series of binary decisions. Take options and compare two at a time until there's only one left. But do it quickly. This way, you only ever have to choose between two options. So pair the options up, and start a rapid process of elimination. This comes into play with company name selection, domain name searching, and a lot of other things in those early days.

I spent four days thinking of my company's name. Like many new business owners, back then, I thought it was also important to have a tagline or slogan. Now, I advise new entrepreneurs not to worry about that because it can eat up a lot of time. So, the original slogan for the company was "modern thought, big picture thinking." I chose the name "Modmacro" because it combines those ideas: "mod" for modern and "macro" for big picture. But if you were to put all of Modmacro's clients in one room and ask how many know of, or have ever heard that line, I can just about guarantee there won't be a single one. The truth is, nobody cares. For small businesses, the existence or absence of a slogan or tagline, whether great, good, or bad, will have no effect of their success.

On the topic of names, I also recommend you carefully balance your ideas before making your final decision. A name that you think is edgy and cool today might not be so great in 10 years. Avoid trendy names and time-sensitive naming conventions, because trends fade quickly. Avoid odd punctuation and capitalization combinations as well. For example, we originally wrote Modmacro as modMACRO. I know it's dumb now, but back then I thought it was cool. But you can't write names that way on legal documents, corporate paperwork, bank documents, etc. So eventually I was forced to drop that foolish uppercase/lowercase style.

For many new business owners, imagining their company ten years down the road seems impossible. After all, they're focused on launching their startup. Sustained growth and years of success aren't usually on the radar yet. That's okay, but assume you'll be using the same company name for a long time, and give that decision its due attention. The same goes for domain names, product names, etc. Balance that with the reality that you can't burn 3 weeks playing with names. Don't let something like a name be the reason your business never gets started at all.

╫ Jessica: When Maven was in its infancy, my original partner and I spent tons of time brainstorming. We were so excited about the whole idea, we would get on the phone for hours and talk about all the different directions we could go with the business. In retrospect, everything we came up with was a great idea for a business, but to try to do all of it would have been insane.

In the end, I think we overwhelmed ourselves even before we got started. It was only in the weeks before we launched that we had real conversations about narrowing our scope and focusing ourselves on the core of the business. By the time we got down to it, we'd almost forgotten our original vision, so going back to it was a little foreign. Don't get me wrong—going down that train of thought was a great exercise in thinking about what the future could hold, but it was too much for our brains to handle that early in the process.

Every now and then, I think about those early conversations, and I believe the business could branch into one of those directions eventually, but now more than ever, I see the need to stick to a clearly defined niche for a while. There is still so much to learn, and we needed to solidify our foundation before taking on anything else.

Options are traditionally seen as a good thing. As humans, we like being able to see choices, and we like being able to compare and contrast them. In starting a business, a little bit of this is vital. You need ideas, and you need creativity. Just be careful not to let the options overwhelm you to the point where you become frozen.

You May Have the Urge to Do Tons of Research

As you're brainstorming and having creative bursts of energy, you may find yourself wanting to research anything and everything you can get your hands on that relates to your ideas. Research is good! It's downright necessary. It would be reckless to start a business without doing any research at all.

Take advantage of your desire to learn. Find reliable sources for the information you need, and seek out what you need to know. Talk to people in your industry. Talk to owners of businesses you frequent. Look for industry-related publications. Seek out forums and websites that can help you answer any questions you have.

Research should be fun. If you don't love the industry you're starting a business in, then you probably should re-think whether it's the right business for you. Researching your industry should energize you and get you excited. Business research is serious, but it can also be enjoyable and rewarding. Time spent on learning is time well spent.

The only time research becomes a waste of time is when it's a roadblock to progress. When you find yourself saying, "I know _____ is the next step, and I know what I should do, but I want to do more research first," that could be a red flag. What's really stopping you from taking that next step? Didn't you already say that you know what to do? Is fear getting in the way?

One of the ways to keep research productive is to have goals. Keep your searches specific and on-topic. Try to limit going down rabbit holes that aren't related to your original search. In your research, you will uncover things you hadn't originally thought of or intended to find, and that's good, but it's up to you to be disciplined about how much time you can spend in this stage before moving on.

Another pitfall of research is that it can be overwhelming. Just like "analysis paralysis," too much information in these early stages can bring you to a screeching halt. The more you learn, the more you realize you don't know, and you can begin to lose confidence very quickly.

There comes a point where you know enough to take the next step, and you just have to do it. You'll learn more as you go, but you have to take that step first. After all, many aspects of business ownership can only be learned by doing. So ask yourself these questions as you perform research: What was my original question or the piece of information I needed? Have I found it?

Once you have, move on.

You'll never know everything, and you will make mistakes. That is one of those harsh facts of entrepreneurship. It's important to embrace that early on so that you can begin to see each mistake as an opportunity to learn more. You can't predict those kinds of learning opportunities by just doing research. You need to move forward and get your hands a little dirty.

Even experienced and successful entrepreneurs admit to trying and failing constantly. And most agree that the best thing you can do is to just get started and see what happens. Mistakes are a normal part of the process. Take Niklas Zennström, co-founder of Skype, for example. He sums it up pretty well: "I make mistakes most of the time, and that's part of the risk profile being an entrepreneur. I guess one big mistake I did was not to start my own company earlier." Don't let research become an excuse for inaction. If you're so afraid of mistakes that you're afraid to start, you may not be cut out for running your own business.

╫ Matt: Some things should really only be done to 90% completion, and here's why: that last 10% can take you a disproportionately large amount of time to achieve. So take the time to do 90% of the research, and then stop. You could learn 10% more, but the time it would take would be paralyzing. Attempting to achieve near-perfection is a waste of time. And at this stage, you need to keep moving quickly and capitalize on that momentum.

My close friend, Matt Grisafe, the owner of AV Programming Associates, uses the phrase "kill the engineer" to illustrate this concept. Engineers are often very smart, perfection-driven people, and they can recognize when a project could be just a little bit better. But if the project is doing the job it's supposed to do, the client is happy, and the timeline is met, then it's done.

Kill the engineer.

There's always room for improvement and perfection can't be achieved, so without the discipline to stop when you should, it can go on forever. We use this saying all the time. Kill the engineer, kill the designer, kill the writer, etc. It's a good reminder to keep around.

I'm not saying don't aim high, but when you've done your due diligence and reached the point of knowing enough to move on, you just need to move on. Kill the engineer, or in this case, kill the researching entrepreneur, and move your business forward.

╫ Jessica: I know this problem all too well. The publishing industry is always changing, and it's hard to stay on top of all the latest information. When we were figuring out some of the first actions we needed to take in getting Maven off the ground, we fell down the research rabbit hole more than once. We wanted to make sure we were optimizing everything, and we spent a lot of time looking at how other companies were doing it.

Some of this was extremely useful. I was able to observe what was working for other companies and what wasn't. I made sure to read about some of the changes in the industry as a whole, and I looked for any information I could find about new systems and techniques companies were using.

After a while, we all had just gone too far. The information became overwhelming. Every company was doing things a little bit differently, and everyone was trying different new techniques to see what would work. Nothing was proven. Everyone else was learning by doing, and we were trying to learn from other people's experiments. One day, we would decide to move forward in a certain direction, but then we'd read something about another company the next day, and completely change directions.

Our research was running us in circles. Once Maven was launched, I realized that we could have launched weeks before we actually did. We were stalling in the name of research, and those extra weeks could have been much better spent learning through experience.

You May Feel the Need to Have a Lot of Meetings

Starting a business alone is the right choice for some, but for others, working with a partner or with a group of people is more desirable. There's no right or wrong answer, and each option has its advantages and disadvantages. One of the fun aspects of working with others during this ideation stage is that you get to bounce ideas off one another.

Like most things in the ideation stage, tossing ideas back and forth with people you'll be working with should be energizing and fun. Hopefully, you've chosen people you want to work with for a long time, and hopefully they have ideas that are complimentary to your own, but just different enough that they help you think of things in a new way. Getting together with your future partners and co-workers can be exciting, because it gives everyone the opportunity to encourage each other.

Just like the desire to keep researching, the desire to keep brainstorming can be powerful. There's so much to learn, and it's easy to think that just one more meeting will help you get your business to where it needs to be.

As anyone who has ever sat in a meeting can testify, there are productive meetings, and there are unproductive meetings. In a productive meeting, everyone is focused, concise, and working towards a common goal. And there's an agenda. People leave the meeting with new energy, and everyone knows what their next task is.

On the other hand, unproductive meetings are exhausting. People get distracted and bring up non-relevant information. These meetings go on way longer than they need to, and people usually leave in a bad mood. Next steps aren't defined, and the team is no better off after the meeting than before. Sometimes, they're actually worse off.

In the early stages of starting a company, most meetings are exciting. Those early meetings are not usually ones that leave everyone depleted. Still, they can get unproductive very quickly. Communication, brainstorming, and shared learning are all good things, and spending some time thinking about your future success can be motivating. The key is to pay attention to balance. Meetings should inspire action, not be a distraction from it.

A common stereotype is the ambitious group of recent college grads who want to start a company together. They know the basics of what needs to be done to get their business up and running, so they're meeting often to discuss names, mission statements, and business plans. They talk a lot about how they're going to be the next Instagram. Or the next Uber. They're excited and can't wait to get started.

They may have a phenomenal idea, and they may even have the knowledge and skill to pull it off. The problem is that their meetings are starting to look a lot more like parties disguised as meetings. They're doing a lot of talking but not a lot of doing. As time goes on, it becomes obvious that several people in the group are more excited about the idea of starting a business than the actual work of starting a business.

This is not to say that these people have bad intentions, or that they're lazy. It's more a comment on the fact that not everyone really wants to be a business owner. We'll dive deeper into partnerships and co-owners in a later chapter, but these early meetings that you're having with your team can be very telling about who is in it for the long haul and who is not.

Have meetings with your potential team and enjoy them. Just be sure to have a clear agenda for each one and stick to the topics at hand as much as possible. You'll foster better relationships with your team, you'll come up with more solid plans, and you'll ensure that you're using your time effectively.

╫ Matt: Because I started Modmacro on my own, I never had the opportunity to fall into the trap of long, unproductive meetings with team members or investors. I took the company from an idea to having clients in less than 30 days. But for the first few years, I really missed having some sort of partner to bounce ideas around with. It's valuable to have a colleague who is both interested and somehow invested in your success who can be a sounding board. If you have that, I strongly recommend taking advantage of it. If not, seek out advisors or develop relationships with businesses you respect that are willing to be a sounding board. Personally, I provide that service to quite a few people. I enjoy being there to listen and being able to offer advice; I very often learn from those conversations as well.

As my team has grown, I've enjoyed being able to work with them, to gain feedback on ideas, and develop goals. It's especially valuable because they are deeply involved in the company and the implementation of the ideas we settle on, and therefore invested in the conversation. With regard to avoiding long, unproductive meetings, that burden falls mostly on me. Of everyone on the team, it turns out I'm the talker, and sometimes I talk too much.

Before starting Modmacro, I was the director of a small software company. We had a team of programmers, and we met each week to review projects. In many cases, it was my responsibility to conduct those meetings and keep them on track. I found that creating and sticking to a specific agenda was key to being efficient, and it's best to have a specific start and end time. Then as the meeting progresses, you can evaluate how far through the agenda you are and how much time is left. Pick up the pace when you need to or slow down when you have time to dig in a little on issues that affect the whole team. Lastly, when side conversations arise, push those off until after the meeting and only include the individuals that are directly involved. Let everyone else get back to work.

╫ Jessica: I was so excited when it finally sunk in that I was going to be running a business. It was terrifying, too, but mostly exciting. All the possibilities started hitting me at once, and I couldn't wait to talk to my partner at the time about where we'd be in a year, five years, or even ten years. In addition to our massive brainstorming sessions, we spent a lot of time on the phone just being excited.

In a way, I'm glad we did that. It kept us energized, even as we went through times where we didn't know what we were doing or when we hit roadblocks. But, I'll be the first to admit that we probably got a little carried away. It's not that what we were doing was bad or wrong; it's just that the time could have been so much better spent. We could have buckled down and figured out clearer and more specific action steps while we were talking. If we'd done that, we would have launched weeks, and possibly months, earlier.

People Will Question Your Idea, and Some Will Even Tell You to Give Up

This can be one of the hardest parts for a would-be business owner, especially someone who is embarking on the adventure for the first time. We all want support, and we hope that the people closest to us will be our biggest cheerleaders. Sadly, this is hardly ever true. There will always be people in your life that will shoot down your idea and tell you why you can't do it.

Most entrepreneurs will tell you: You need to have thick skin and a little touch of crazy. Chances are, you're trying to do something that no one else is doing, so of course there are going to be people who aren't as optimistic as you are. They probably have good intentions, but their fears for you are not facts. You cannot let any of that get to you.

Once again, you cannot let any of that get to you.

People handle negativity from others in a variety of ways. Some people take that negativity and become ultra-motivated to prove the naysayers wrong. That attitude can be helpful because it makes it easier to push through in the face of adversity. It can also be a little scary because in an effort to stick it to people who aren't supporting you, you can easily overlook actual problems. It's often said that "attitude is everything," but balance is important, too.

On the other hand, some people hear negativity from people they expected to be supportive, and they crumble. They lose confidence, and they start questioning even the most basic decisions. This is tragic and crippling.

In the worst-case scenario, your idea really is crazy and doomed to failure. If you had the opportunity to survey every successful entrepreneur in the world, most of them will tell you about past failures. Failure is never the goal, but it is rarely the big, scary result it's made out to be. Failure can be a powerful learning experience, and for some people, failure is nothing but an early step towards success.

✠ Matt: Entrepreneurs have to know in their heart that self-doubt is normal and healthy, as is listing to trusted advisors. But you're nothing as an entrepreneur if you don't know when to push forward regardless of external voices. Sometimes that's just what it takes. Think about the position of an entrepreneur. This is a person who, by definition, is staking their success or failure on the idea that they can create something from nothing, captivate the market, sell and deliver products or services, carve out success in a noisy space, and sometimes, do it alone. If this isn't you, stay with your nine to five job and be happy.

✠ Jessica: I've often thought I could run a business, and mainly for the reasons we've mentioned. I've seen things done poorly, and I've felt I have the skills to do them better. However, I don't come from a family of entrepreneurs, nor did I grow up with a circle of friends who wanted to be entrepreneurs. I was taught to favor safety and security, so when I started doing my own thing, a lot of people around me got concerned.

The best advice I can give is simply that if you want it, you need to go after it. You might fail, but that possibility should be exhilarating and motivating. If the thought of failure is so frightening that it's insurmountable, then it's possible entrepreneurship isn't for you. It's never going to feel comfortable, and I don't know a single entrepreneur who feels confident 100% of the time. That nagging sense of questioning and self-doubt is what keeps you sharp and tuned in to your business.

Don't quit unless you want to quit, no matter what anyone tells you.

Final Thoughts About Stage One

A LOT OF WHAT we've covered so far applies to any hopeful entrepreneur with any business idea. Anyone thinking about starting a business will go through most, if not all, of the thoughts and issues we've talked about.

From this point forward, you will need to start thinking very specifically about your business idea and answering some of the hard questis that will lead you towards launch. The next four questions will get you thinking about your business and about what kind of planning lies ahead in the next stage.

Does your business idea fill a hole in the market and solve a need or problem people have?

Ideally, you want your business to do something that no one else is already doing. At the very least, you want to make sure you're doing it in a way that sets you apart from anyone else who may already have had the same idea.

On the other side of that is the fact that not every novel or original idea is a necessary one. People have ideas for businesses all the time, and one of the most important questions they need to eventually ask themselves is, "who is my customer?" We'll get into that in greater detail in the next stage, but if you literally cannot think of anyone who would need your product or service, you're in trouble.

Even if your target niche seems small, make sure there's at least someone who will need what you're trying to create.

Is there a lot of competition for the business you're starting?

A little competition can be good; a lot of competition could be a problem. The truth is: starting out is hard anyway, even if you're the only one doing what you do. Jumping into the deep end with a lot of established businesses can make it that much harder.

You'll have to decide whether the risk of entering into a highly competitive market is worth it, and your answer may depend on the industry you're going into. Looking at question one again can help. If the product or service you're offering is a huge need in the world, then you can still have success among a lot of competition. Your focus will just have to be on differentiating your business and making it stand out from the rest.

With a Starbucks, Peet's, or Caribou Coffee on practically every corner in America, it seems insane to open a small local coffee shop. But coffee is something that people love, and many buy it every single day. It has become a ritual for many. Moreover, people love the consistency and comfort of their favorite shop, but they are often willing to try something new if the products and services are outstanding.

You can get into the coffee industry if you are offering a superior experience, and if you take your time to choose the right location. Local coffee shops are popping up everywhere, and it's starting to disrupt the industry a little. It's an exciting time for the smaller guys in the coffee shop world.

On the other hand, look at bookstores. People love to read, but with the way the industry has changed over the last decade, people are shifting away from bookstores and towards online retail giants like Amazon. When there used to be a Borders, a Barnes & Noble, or a Waldenbooks in every mall or shopping center, many of those are gone. Barnes & Noble is the only one of those three companies still standing, and many believe they are on their last leg.

In the bookstore industry, the small businesses aren't faring well either. The number of independent bookstores in the United States dropped from 2,400 to 1,900 between 2002 and 2011, and the number continues to fall. It may seem like a good time to jump into the industry because the competition is decreasing, but there's a reason for that. People just aren't buying books like they used to.

Is your idea scalable?

Scalability is a word you'll hear a lot from other business owners and investors. Essentially, does your business idea leave room for growth? Growth isn't the only measure of success, but it's certainly important. Some people create their business with the idea that they want to "stay small," but you can still scale while remaining a small business.

If there is no way for your business to scale at all, you are going to run into problems very quickly. You'll be standing in your way and limiting your own success. Even just the basics of inflation will affect your life, and the only way to cope with that is to be more successful in your business and bring in higher profits.

You can think about the "hows" later, but you need to at least see possibility for growth. It doesn't have to be large growth or fast growth, but stagnation is not an option.

Have you done any basic market research?

Market research is a big component of getting your business started. You need to understand the demand for your product or service, and you need to have some understanding of who your customers will be. If you're building a brick and mortar business, you need to put some time into researching the right location to serve your core customers. If you're building a business that can essentially be run over the internet, you still need to know who your customers are and how to reach them.

You do not need to already have a detailed business plan written at this stage, but some very basic market research will help you tremendously as you start to make concrete plans for your future business.

If you're still with us, you must be ready to move on into the next stage. This is where things get a little bit more serious and where you need to begin to make some decisions. In this stage, you'll go through all of the different components of your business, and you'll lay the foundation for launch.

Because you're still making plans at this point, you'll have to leave some room for flexibility, as things change leading up to launch and shortly after your business gets off the ground. Still, you want to go through this next section carefully and be as specific as possible in your plans. The more prepared you are, the better you'll be able to handle surprises and setbacks.

Stage Two: Planning

The Business Plan

BUSINESS PLANS. YOU love 'em, or you hate 'em. Some people insist that you cannot start a business before writing a proper, detailed business plan. We are not those people. We know you can start a successful business without one because we've both done it.

There are some instances in which a business plan is absolutely necessary. If you're trying to get funding from investors or trying to secure a business loan from a bank, you will need to provide a complete business plan. However, to just get up and running, a perfectly formed business plan is not a requirement.

That said, we still think it's important to go through many of the steps of forming a business plan, even if you don't take the time to write it all down and properly format it. Every piece of information in a business plan is vital, and just going through the process of thinking about all of those pieces can help you down the road.

Here are the parts of a business plan in a little more detail, and how each can help you think more clearly about your business so that you get off to a solid start. The Executive Summary

In a formal, written business plan, this is the first section. It is essentially a summary of all of the pertinent information about your business, allowing investors, bankers, etc., to get a quick glance into your business and your goals. An executive summary should be exactly that—a summary—which means it should be less than a page long. It should include a description of the business including products, services, and target market; key financial information including sales numbers, margins, and desired capital; legal components of the business including personnel and form of operation; and any major achievements the business has had to date.

If you're actually writing up a formal business plan, don't get stuck on the executive summary. Draw up the rest of the business plan first, and pull the key points for the summary last.

If you're simply using the business plan framework for your own clarification about your business, an executive summary may not be a necessary step.

The Business Description

This is where the real meat of the business plan begins. In your business description, you need to go into all of the details of your business, starting with your industry. Information about market conditions, developments or new products within the industry, and your specific niche is important to any potential investors or lenders, but this is also vital information for you as the business owner. Even if you're not formalizing a plan for investors and outside parties, you need to have a thorough understanding of the industry you're about to enter.

Along with industry research, a good business description should include information about the structure of the business, the target market, the products or services it will be providing, and how your business will stand out among competitors.

Finally, describe how your business will make money. Where will revenue come from, and how will you become profitable? Again, investors and lenders obviously want to know this, but you need to know this, too. Many business owners begin working on their ideas with great intentions of solving consumer problems or providing needed services, but they forget that profitability is the key to long-term sustainability.

The Market Analysis

Market research, like industry research, is incredibly important. A full market analysis is an involved process, but is necessary if you are presenting your business plan to investors. They are going to want to know every detail about the state of the market, your target and feasible markets, your competition and how your business is different, the potential for market growth as a whole and the growth potential for your business within the market, your pricing strategy, your plans for promotion and positioning, your distribution strategy, and your sales projections.

That is a lot of information, but all of it is helpful. If you have aspirations to grow your business and continue to be successful over time, you're going to need to understand what's happening in the market and how your business fits in. By the time you're putting together a business plan, it's no longer enough to make guesses and assumptions about the market. As the great statistician W. Edwards Deming said, "Without data, you're just another person with an opinion."

The key is to not become overwhelmed at this point. We mentioned analysis paralysis in the first section. It's important to realize that industry and market research can both be time-consuming endeavors, and you could probably spend the rest of your life on research if you allowed yourself. Don't get stuck here! Do your due diligence, and be aware that it's impossible to know everything.

Also know that market research never ends. As your business gets up and running, you'll see changes in the market, and you'll need to adjust. You want to understand the state of the market as completely as possible when you launch, but recognize that you'll be constantly looking at this kind of data as you grow. In other words, there will be plenty of opportunities to shift or change course if you happen to overlook something at the beginning.

The Design and Development Plan

Up to this point, you've been answering the "what" and "why" questions about your business, but in this part of the business plan, you begin to answer the "how." A design and development plan requires you to think about how you'll develop and market your products or services, and how you'll run your business from an organizational standpoint.

As with every part of a business plan, the level of detail you put into this section is dependent on your purpose. If you're presenting this plan to investors or lenders, they are going to want to see that you've thought out your development processes thoroughly, and that you have step-by-step plans that you intend to follow. They'll want to see a timeline and a budget for each step so that they know that they'll see a return on their investment.

This is another place in the business plan where you can get really bogged down with details and stall out. Based on your business description, you should have a good handle on the products and/or services you'll be offering, but if you don't know every tiny procedural detail, that's okay. You will figure some things out as you go, and that's completely normal for a new business owner. Even those who plan things in a very specific way often find that things change once they get started.

The main point here is that plotting a course for development is a useful exercise, but don't let every single "how" stop you from moving forward.

The Financial Statements

A formal business plan always includes a few key financial documents: income statements, balance sheets, and cash flow documents. Again, the main purpose of this is so that investors and lenders can assess the health of your business plan and calculate their risk.

As we stated in the beginning of this book, you may be in any one of several situations. If you've been in business for a while, but are finding yourself back in startup mode for whatever reason, then these financial documents should be easy to find and review. And you should review them. If you're back in startup mode, that's an indicator that some things need to change, and you need to know your numbers forwards and backwards if you're going to be making changes to your business.

For those of you who haven't started your business yet, nailing down the financial information can seem like an almost impossible task. You're going to have to make some projections, and that's hard to do when you haven't gotten up and rolling yet. Like with all of these sections, don't let the unknown paralyze you. For the sake of potential investors, you'll need to have specifics (even though they're just projections), and you'll need to back your numbers up with solid research.

That is the important thing to remember here. If you've done your due diligence in your research and developmental planning, you should have some reliable financial projections to work with, and that will help you immensely as you get your business started.

Business plans can be daunting, especially if you've never written one before. There is a lot of information that needs to be covered in the plan, but don't feel like you have to wing it. There are many guides out there that can provide you with templates and walkthroughs to create a formal business plan. Entrepreneur Magazine (www.entrepreneur.com) and the US Small Business Administration (www.sba.gov) both have excellent resources regarding business plans and what to include.

╫ Matt: Formal business plans certainly have their place. But they aren't always necessary, and can often become a hindrance to launching the business.

I started Modmacro like most small business owners. I funded it myself and started small. So for me, a formal plan would have been a waste of time. I did a lot of research to understand the market and worked quickly to identify our differentiating factors. I also established short-term financial goals related to revenue and profitability for immediately after launch. Specifically, I set 90-day and six-month goals. Then, I watched my progress closely with those goals as the metric.

If you're looking for financing of any type, you'll have to develop a great business plan to present. But if you're not, I recommend only developing a complete written plan if your business model is complex or if you've got multiple people involved. One thing I know is that it's almost impossible to keep multiple people on the same page if you don't have the key points written down.

Unfortunately, we often see the business plan act as a major impediment to getting started. Sometimes people feel strongly that they need it, when they probably don't. If you're starting a simple business and it's just you, then you're making a mistake spending a month on the business plan. Often this becomes an excuse to wait before spending money on professional services. Some first-time entrepreneurs struggle to build enough confidence to move forward until they have a massive plan in place, even though nobody will ever see the plan.

The most important thing to keep in mind is that everything you do pre-launch is theoretical. Therefore, most of it will evolve as you gain experience and interact with the market. So make the best plans you can with the information you have. Just be open to improving the plan as you gather new information, and recognize that for the life of your business, that cycle never ends.

╫ Jessica: We definitely did not write any kind of formal business plan for Maven before getting started. We weren't looking for loans or investors, and it didn't seem like creating a business plan would be beneficial. To us, it was more important to just get going, and we figured we'd learn along the way. Plus, Maven's business model is very simple, and it seemed like working up a formal business plan would only complicate things.

For Maven, this was probably the right decision, and here's why: we still did a lot of planning, even though it wasn't in the shape of a true-to-form business plan. We thought about all of the things outlined above, but in a broader way than a business plan would require. We left ourselves a lot of room for flexibility, and we allowed ourselves to be okay with the fact that we didn't have all the answers.

Whether or not to create a business plan is something every business owner needs to decide. There are scenarios in which it may be absolutely necessary (seeking investors), and there are scenarios in which taking that much time to plan could be a roadblock. I think it's important to know what a business plan is so that you know the kinds of things you should be thinking about as you start your business, but I also think it's important to keep moving and not let the details kill your momentum.

The Mission Statement

LIKE BUSINESS PLANS, mission statements are another controversial topic among entrepreneurs. Do you really need one before you get your business started? Do you even need one at all? If you ask 100 entrepreneurs these questions, you'll probably get as many answers, or at least that many definitions of the meaning and purpose of a mission statement

In order to figure out if you should spend time working on a mission statement at this stage, it's important to first understand what a mission statement is and what purpose it serves. According to many business how-tos, a mission statement should be a concise statement (200 words or less, ideally) that conveys what your business is, what you're offering your customers, who your customers are, what your company's values are, and what makes you stand out.

That's a lot to cram into 200 words, and if you've ever tried to write a clear and concise summary of anything, you know how difficult it can be. Now try and take your business and describe it in 200 words. Many people struggle with this, and it can delay you indefinitely if you're insistent on writing a mission statement before launching your business.

This is not a criticism of mission statements. Mission statements can be powerful, both for a company and its customers. Having a central vision that you can refer to on a daily basis can be helpful in boosting morale and in making tough decisions whenever your business faces crossroads.

The important thing to remember is that your mission statement before you launch may look different than it does in the weeks, months, and first few years after you launch. As your business finds its place in the market, things will change, and you may find yourself with different goals and values than you started with.

Not all companies need a proper mission statement. Some of the top companies in the world don't have one that includes everything listed above. Look at Starbucks. Their mission is: "to inspire and nurture the human spirit—one person, one cup, and one neighborhood at a time." It's a lovely sentiment, and it speaks to the passion they have for their customers. However, it doesn't say anything specific about coffee or tea, it doesn't specify who their customers are, and it says nothing about standing out.

Yet, it's effective. No one would disagree that Starbucks's mission statement is a reflection of their brand. It's also important to note that their current mission statement was only written recently—in 2008. They've refined their mission statement over the years as they've seen the industry change, and as they've shifted their goals from being a product-focused brand to being a community-focused brand. CEO Howard Schultz says, "The success of Starbucks demonstrates the fact we have built an emotional connection with our customers. . . Our people have done a wonderful job of knowing your drink, your name, your kids' names, and what you do for a living." He couldn't have known that Starbucks would become such an emotional brand back in 1971 when all they wanted to do was provide customers with better coffee.

It's a good thing to have some kind of statement that unifies your company and your goals. Just be aware that it can change over time, and that you need not have the perfect mission statement to get started. In fact, you can start your business without any mission statement at all. If you need some help figuring out if you should have a mission statement, or if you need help focusing one you've already written, there some excellent articles and resources in Businessing Magazine (www.businessingmag.com).

╫ Matt: Many small businesses evolve the mission statement (or at least the implementation of the mission statement) rapidly in the first year or so. Be okay with knowing what you're about, but ready to adapt to what the market tells you works and what doesn't.

At Modmacro, we place a lot of value on having a documented mission statement. I find it a practical tool to use as a grid that we run decisions through. Without having a defined mission, how do you know when something is off mission? However, agonizing over the development of a mission statement before you even launch may not be the best way to spend your time.

When we launched the company in 2010, our list of digital marketing services was limited. Over the years, we've incrementally expanded what we do. So the fact that I didn't develop a formal mission statement on day one was not an issue. That said, there are certain core elements that were established before we launched and have not changed to this day.

For instance, our target audience hasn't changed at all. We continue to be laser focused on partnering with small businesses and non-profits. Likewise, many of the components to our approach have remained the same. For example, I intentionally limit the size of the company to ensure our clients continue to receive the boutique experience they crave.

These days we do have a formal mission statement, which we revisit annually. While all the pieces of our mission statement are communicated across our website, the whole statement isn't published anywhere as a complete entity. We didn't think that was necessary.

╫ Jessica: Maven's mission statement, "A boutique publishing house of non-fiction, making published authors out of entrepreneurs, business people, and professionals," is close to the traditional definition of a mission statement. It says who we are, a boutique publishing house; what we provide, non-fiction publishing; and whom we provide it to, entrepreneurs, business people, and professionals. For us, it was important to be specific so that we would know how to effectively market our services.

That mission statement didn't come easy, though. A lot of time and back-and-forth went into creating it. There was probably an entire week where my original partner and I emailed each other ideas about how we wanted our business to operate and the various values that were important to us. I don't want to say that it was wasted time, because it was helpful to know that we were working towards the same vision, but at the same time, that week could have probably been used more effectively. We did a lot of talking and not a lot of doing.

I also think we were wrong in thinking that we absolutely had to come up with a mission statement before launching. It has ended up being a prominent feature on our website, so I'm glad we have it, but in retrospect, I don't think we needed to have that set in stone before we started marketing ourselves and taking clients.

I liken it a little to writing books. Having a rough outline before getting started can be helpful, because it can give you focus and direction. However, spending a bunch of time on a well-crafted, perfectly-succinct synopsis before getting started would be a waste of time, especially if it causes you to get stuck. The direction of the story could change as you start writing, and then you'd have to go back and change the synopsis anyway.

My advice: have a vision, but leave room for flexibility. And whatever you do, don't let a lack of the "perfect" mission statement keep you from launching your business.

Identifying Your
Target Customer

THERE'S A FAMOUS line from the movie *Field of Dreams*: "If you build it, he will come," and it has been interpreted by many aspiring business owners as, "If I start this business, customers will appear." If it were truly that simple, then we'd have no need for the estimated $62 billion digital marketing industry or the hundreds of millions of dollars spent by companies worldwide on advertising. Obviously, there is a little more strategy involved in getting customers to buy your products and services.

What you need to think about as an entrepreneur, especially if this is your first business, is the fact that you're going to appeal more to some people than others. Certain age groups, genders, professionals, and people with specific interests are more likely to become customers of your specific business, and your marketing efforts will be the most effective if you target those people.

Figuring out your target market is a big part of market research and the market analysis you do while you're creating a business plan, and the process can vary, depending on what type of business you are building.

For example, if you're opening a neighborhood vegan restaurant, your market research might initially be based on location. Who are the people in the local area who might be interested in high-quality meals that are free of animal products? Whereas, if you're opening an online handcrafted custom jewelry shop, location is not nearly as important, because your customers can be anywhere with an internet connection. You'll need to focus on other factors like age and lifestyle to narrow down the profile of your target customer.

One approach to identifying your target customers is to start as specific as possible, and expand from there. Build the most detailed profile you can think of, and include everything from basic demographic information to location, hobbies, spending habits, income, lifestyle, and values. Once you know exactly who that person is, you can begin to widen your lens on some of the characteristics and identify patterns that will help you reach a bigger audience as you grow.

Another approach to take, or even something you can do as you're thinking about the demographics of your target customers, is to consider who they are as people. If you could choose the types of people you work with, how would they act? How would they treat you and your company? What would your relationship look like?

That may sound very abstract and difficult to define, but it can make an enormous difference. When you first launch your business, you'll have a sense of desperation. You'll be happy to work with anyone who wants to work with you. That's normal for a business that has just opened its doors. That said, as you consider your potential for growth and as you think about how you want your company to take shape, it helps to have those ideal customers in mind right from the very beginning. Thinking this way will help you steer your marketing efforts in a productive direction.

For example, a friend of ours, Mark Grisafe, is the owner of M. Grisafe Architect, a small architecture firm in the Long Beach, California area. After being in business for over a decade, he realized that not much had changed since he first began. He was working one job after another, but something just wasn't clicking. He wasn't finding a great connection with some of his clients, and he wanted to attract more business, but also the right kind of business. He came to Modmacro for help, thinking that marketing would be the answer.

As it turned out, marketing was the answer, but not in the way you probably think. When Mark really sat down and thought about it, what he realized he needed to do was spend some time analyzing his ideal client. He'd been noticing the types of jobs that had been the most rewarding to him over the years, and he'd taken note of the types of clients he most enjoyed working with. Analyzing them demographically wasn't much help because they had as many differences as similarities. What was helpful, however, was analyzing their attitudes.

Mark discovered that he wanted more clients who wanted to be intimately involved in the design process. He wanted to work with people who would be as passionate about their new facility, office, or addition to their home, as he would be about designing it. As a bonus, he discovered that clients who behaved this way were actually less budget-conscious and less likely to complain about pricing.

For those of you about to start a business for the first time, you may be thinking, "How can I know what attitude I want my customers to have if I haven't even gotten my first customer yet?" It may take getting a few jobs under your belt before you can recognize the subtle differences between the customers who are helping you move your business in the right direction and those who are "just another job." But if you do know the types of customers you're trying to attract, the right kinds of marketing efforts at the start can help you do just that.

For Mark, marketing meant creating content and messaging that communicates his own attitude towards his business and his clients. When potential clients read his blog or his Facebook page, they understand how passionate he is about his work, and they can tell how much he values collaboration and community. Now, people call his office and quote pieces off his website to him. They let him know that his message is coming across. His ideal clients are finding him because he has clearly and publicly defined exactly who he is looking for.

Defining your target customer can be tricky. There are a lot of factors to consider. It's important to spend some time with it in this planning stage so you can market yourself efficiently and start gaining traction in your industry. As time goes on, you'll receive more feedback from customers, and you'll learn more about yourself as a business owner. As your business matures, you'll get better and better at defining your ideal target market.

╫ Matt: This is one area where having competitors is a good thing. Look at what successful companies are doing and how they attract the right customers. Now merge that with your plan and mission to reach those same people in your unique way, or even find segments of the target that are underserved or ignored by larger competitors. Attract those people.

It's important to recognize any potential barriers to customers understanding what you do. If you're the first to market on a new idea, you'll almost certainly have the challenge of not only reaching people, but also educating them on what you offer. On the other hand, if there are lots of competitors, then it's likely that the public already understands the need you're filling.

╫ Jessica: At Maven, we wanted to be specific about our target customer because there are a lot of publishing companies out there, some good and some not so good. By narrowing our marketing efforts and identifying exactly who would benefit the most from our services, we are able to differentiate ourselves from some of the other companies out there.

We did a lot of research into other publishing companies, both big and small, to see who they were targeting and why. Ultimately, we found that there was a big hole in the market for exactly what we were trying to do. No one was specifically looking to help entrepreneurs and professionals publish books that would help them position themselves in their industries. In that respect, we got a little bit lucky.

Our work is not done, though. Especially in terms of marketing, we are constantly looking at data from our website and social media profiles to see who is paying attention to us. We've been contacted by a handful of people who are pretty far outside what I would consider our original target, and that's very interesting to us. We're looking at patterns and tweaking our marketing efforts to make sure we're taking advantage of opportunities we hadn't initially thought of, while still staying on mission.

It's an evolving process, and probably always will be. I think it would have been crazy to try and launch without identifying who we believed would be interested in our services. This is a step that cannot be skipped, in my opinion.

Defining and Developing Your Product or Service

FOR MANY BUSINESS owners, the product or service is what drives the whole business idea from the beginning. Chances are, you've put a lot of thought into what you plan to sell and how you plan to sell it. Now that you're seriously planning your business and you're on your way to launching, it's time to revisit your ideas and make them as specific as possible.

Here are some things you need to think about as you figure out what your business will be providing to its customers and where your revenue will come from. What is Your Product/Service?

This sounds like such a simple question, but the more detailed and specific you can be at this stage, the better. For example, if you're opening a neighborhood pet store, what kinds of pet products will you have? Toys? Food? Beds? Small animal habitats? Which animals will you have products for? Dogs? Cats? Exotic pets? Birds? Will you sell any animals or provide any adoption services? Will you offer training classes? What will you have in your store that will make customers choose you over one of the larger pet stores like PetSmart or Petco?

You can be very specific in a service-oriented business, too. Take a photography business, for example: What subject material do you specialize in? Will you do custom/commissioned work? Will you photograph special events? Will you have a gallery of prints for sale?

As you start gaining customers, you may end up refining your product or service further. You may find that there's a high demand for something you weren't originally offering, or you may find the opposite—that there's a certain item or service people aren't as interested in as you thought they'd be. You can make adjustments as your business grows, but it is vital to start somewhere. You need specific plans in place in order to get to the next stage.

How is Your Product Manufactured, Created, or Acquired?

For product-oriented businesses, it's time to start thinking about the product manufacturing and/or the buying process. You may not be at the point where you've actually reached out to manufacturers or vendors yet, but you should definitely be making a list of possibilities. If you plan to manufacture your products in-house, make a list of equipment you'll need, and start making a plan for acquiring any tools you don't already have.

You may also need to hire a design or engineering team, depending on your product. Technology startups often bring in highly skilled developers and programmers who specialize in designing apps, software programs, and even hardware components. If you have an idea for a product, but aren't sure how to execute it, this is the time to think about contacting professionals who can help you. It's an upfront expense, and it may take designers or developers some time to refine the product and make it perfect, but it's important to get it right.

Service-oriented businesses have less to think about here, but it's still important to identify any equipment or tools that will be needed to provide the services you intend to offer. Back to the example of a photography business: A photographer may need to buy different cameras, lenses, backdrops, props, or editing software.

This is the time to start thinking about the cost of goods, also. There is a balance when it comes to cost, quality, and profit margins, and it's never too soon to start figuring that piece out. If you've already reached out to manufacturers and vendors, you may have received a few quotes to work with. If you haven't made contact yet, you should still be able to make some educated estimations, based on your research.

Understanding how much it will cost for you to make or acquire your products will help you as you start to think about pricing.

How Much Will You Sell Your Product/Service For?

The pricing discussion can be a complicated one, and it can be a source of great stress, especially for first-time entrepreneurs. Even experienced business owners struggle with pricing decisions from time to time, which is why Matt was inspired to write an entire chapter about it in his first book, *Kill the Noise*.

In our research for this book, Matt shared the following story about his father, and how he came to understand pricing and perceived value:

Growing up, I spent a lot of time at car shows and swap meets with my dad. He was always building cars and buying and selling parts. When I was nine, we were at an annual event in San Diego where we had a regular stall in the parking lot of Jack Murphy Stadium, now named Qualcomm Stadium. By regular, I mean we had the same spot each year. We were near the E3 section and occupied one of the more than 19,000 parking spaces in the lot. Our neighboring sellers were also long-time regulars, and therefore friends of my father's. At various times throughout the day my dad would leave me in charge of selling so he could wander the swap meet looking for more parts to buy, and the neighbors would keep an eye on me.

This particular year is the one I best remember because that's when I learned about perceived value. One of the items my dad was selling was a flyball governor from a small turn-of-the-century steam engine. On Friday, he was asking for $60 for it. On Saturday, he continued asking for $60. But he pointed out to me how many people had shown interest in the part. They would pick it up, ask about the price, and then say, "That's in really good shape, and a fair price." Then they would put it down and move on.

Later on Saturday, my dad commented that he didn't know why the governor wasn't selling. People continued to show interest, agreed it was a good piece, and agreed the price was reasonable; but nobody was buying it. He jokingly theorized that maybe people just weren't that impressed because the price was too reasonable. At the time, I didn't really understand that idea. But the next day, while my dad was out walking around, I decided to test his theory. When the first person asked about the governor, I told them a little about it, commented that it was in great shape, and gave them a price of $90. They bought it without hesitation.

When my dad returned, he was impressed with what I'd done, and gave me twenty dollars. That day, I learned a lot about pricing, and how people place value. It was the same exact part and the same audience looking at it, but by increasing the price, it caused the buyer to perceive it at a higher value. It's quite stupid when you stop to think about the psychology of how that works, but nevertheless, it's a reality.

I know a lot of small business owners who struggle to price their services. Some use a cost plus model, and some employ more of a market value approach. But few truly understand the importance that price plays on perceived value. Consider this. What kind of value do you place on free gifts that companies give? Further, how do you perceive the value of a service when you see the company regularly offering deep discounts or coupons? I imagine that in both cases you see less value. Now consider brands like Tiffany & Co., American Express, and BMW. Each of them charges a premium for their products and services. Maybe they're better, maybe they aren't, but do you perceive a higher value in their offerings because you know they are more expensive?

This is not to say that you should overcharge for your products and services, but it is important to recognize the effect price can have on people's buying habits. In your research on the industry and your competition, you have probably come across similar companies to yours that are either over- or undercharging. Try to look at those companies from a consumer's point of view, and think about how you perceive those companies and the quality of what they're offering.

We don't believe there's anything to gain by competing on price alone. Unless your business demands that you beat the competition on pricing (i.e. a discount store), we always recommend charging what your product or service is worth, and doing so unapologetically.

How Will You Sell Your Product/Service?

You surely already know whether you're going to have a brick and mortar location, or if you'll only be conducting business online. It's an important distinction to make, as it will define everything from your general operations to your marketing strategy.

Another thing to think about: Will customers be interfacing directly with your business, either in your location or via your website? Or will you be employing a sales team? A real estate brokerage, for example, relies on a team of individual agents to make sales. They're paid entirely or at least partly on commission, so that is something to factor into your financial projections and possibly even your pricing structure.

Planning out all of the details of your products and services is challenging. It is probably one of the most complicated parts of the planning stage because there are so many details to consider. It's easy to become overwhelmed by all of the options and decisions, but resist the temptation to cut corners. Your products and services are the core of your business, and it's okay to spend some extra time making sure your customers will be getting exactly what you intend for them to get.

Identifying Your Team

IF YOU ARE going to be running your business as a sole proprietor, and no one else is coming on board, then you may not need this section. However, if you are working with even one other person or if you plan to do so in the future, pay attention, because your choices in personnel will affect you daily.

Partnerships

Is there a person or a group of people who have been running alongside you and helping you make crucial decisions? Have you talked to these people about moving forward with you as the business launches? Are they people you think you can work with in the long run? Have you considered co-owning the business with them?

These are conversations you need to have sooner rather than later. Sharing a vision with people, or even one other person, can make running a business more fun, and it can give you the opportunity to see things from perspectives other than your own. It's also highly challenging, especially if not everyone is on the same page about roles, responsibilities, and equity in the business. Feelings can get hurt, tension can become insurmountable, and legal battles can ensue.

So, sit down with anyone working with you right now, and have a serious discussion about vision and goals. When you enter into any kind of partnership or legal entity with other people, it's like a marriage. You may not always agree on everything, but you have to be able to respect each other enough to put the business above personalities, and to make decisions that are best for the business.

If you're going to be splitting equity with anyone, you also need to clearly define everyone's role in the business and set up solid expectations. There cannot be any vagueness about what each person needs to do in order to earn their equity. It's not about being domineering or egotistical—it's about fairness and accountability.

Employees and Contractors

You may have a conversation with the people you're working with right now and find out that they have no interest in becoming partners. They may want to continue working with the business, but as employees or even contractors, rather than as partial owners. Chances are, you'll need other people to fulfill various roles in the company, so this could end up being a blessing. You don't have to worry about the challenges of a partnership, but you still get to work with people who believe in the business, and who have specific skills to make it run well.

If there are roles to fill, and the people you've been working with are not going to be able to fill all of them, you need to think about how you're going to go about finding the right people. Our friend Matthew Grisafe, President of AV Programming Associates has almost always relied on word-of-mouth to fill open positions, and nearly everyone on his team is either someone he already knew personally, or someone specifically referred by another team member. He has found job postings to be far less effective than personal networking.

You may find the opposite to be true. Depending on your industry, there may be a huge pool of talented and qualified people looking for jobs, so forums and job sites may be a good tool for you. Right now, the IT Security industry is boasting a zero percent unemployment rate, meaning anyone in that field who wants a job can get one. As a result, people in that field are jumping around to different companies rather than spending their whole careers in one place. If you're starting a business in the IT Security field, you can probably find dozens of qualified people to round out your team in a relatively short period of time by posting on industry job sites.

As with anything in the planning stage, your team will change over time. People will move on, and some people will have to be let go. It's all part of doing business. Still, you want to start on the right foot and with a strong team that will help you weather the storm of launch. Just remember to communicate clearly, and set expectations upfront. That is the best way to avoid any awkward and messy personnel situations in a brand new business.

✠ Matt: When I first wanted to start a company, I envisioned a small business that I'd run with a buddy. We talked about it, and we found a small niche where mechanical engineering and software programming intersect. We both had jobs, so our plan was to do our business on the side and build it slowly while we kept our jobs. "Dream big, but start small," we said.

What ended up happening, though, is we would each go to work, and then come home and talk about how we wanted to do our own thing. We both knew there was a better way, at least for us, to do business, so we got a little more serious about it. We did one project together, and that was when we realized, "Hey, we can make money doing this!" From that point forward, my goal was to keep pushing and turning it into a full time thing.

That was when everything changed. My buddy sat me down, and we had a realistic conversation about it. He said, "Look, I know you're going to go full force on this, and I know that if I don't work on it 24 hours a day like you will, then you're eventually going to feel like there's an imbalance. You're going to get angry with me, and it's going to kill our friendship. I don't want to do that."

He was right. He had a family, and I was still single at the time, so I had more time to spend on a startup. I understood where he was coming from, because I would have gotten frustrated if he constantly had to put work off because of outside factors. We had a great plan, and the one project we did turned out as well as anyone could have hoped, but we were not the right fit to continue together.

Now, more than ten years later, we have developed successful careers separately, but we are still best friends. We're constantly advising one another.

╫ Jessica: Like Matt, I've experienced a partnership not working out the way I'd planned. Maven was initially a three-way partnership, but as we inched closer to launch, we came to realize that we had differences of opinion and vision that couldn't be reconciled. It came to a point where one person decided that the best thing for him and for his family was to take his career in a different direction.

It was hard because he'd been such an integral part of Maven's concept, original vision, and mission. We owe a lot of Maven's foundation to him and his ideas. It just ultimately wasn't the right combination of people, and we couldn't have moved forward like we were.

Our challenge now, personnel-wise, is to find contractors who are reliable and trainable. We like building strong relationships with people, and we are proud of the fact that most of our contractors have been working with us since the very beginning, or even before Maven was officially launched. As we're growing and taking on more projects, we're finding a need to reach out and find some new people who see our vision and want to rise up to the standard we've set for our products and services.

Final Thoughts About Stage Two

ARE YOU GETTING excited yet? We hope so, because as you move into the next stage, there's no turning back!

Okay, that's not 100% true. You can turn back now and quit if you really want to. If all of this planning has made you realize that you actually *don't* want to be a business owner, then it's far better to cut your losses and get out now before you get in too deep.

This is not meant to be discouraging. Rather, it is to make sure you fully understand what the next stage brings. In the next stage, you will be building relationships with other professionals. You will be signing contracts. You will be creating accounts. You will be doing things that are binding and difficult to get out of. In other words, the ball is already rolling, and it's about to start rolling a lot faster. It probably feels a little bit scary, but it should also be exhilarating.

So, again: Are you excited?

If you are, you're ready.

Let's move on.

Stage Three:
Execution

Putting the Plan into Action

You've gone through a lot to get here. You have been thinking and planning, then thinking and planning some more. You've probably put a few of your thoughts and plans into action, but not very many. Everything up to this point has been mostly theoretical, and not much has been set in stone, if anything.

This is where all of that changes.

Before we get deep into the specific pieces of this stage, we'd like to give you a small thought experiment. This is designed to help you think ahead so that you don't find yourself on launch date panicking and realizing that there are about a hundred things you forgot to do. To be clear—you'll probably forget *something*. No launch day is seamless and perfect; our goal here is simply to minimize the mistakes as much as possible.

The first step in this thought experiment is to set a launch date. Be realistic about it. Choose a target you can actually hit. For most people, that's going to be at least three to four months out. Some of you will be inclined to choose a date that is very far in the future—a year or more away. If you've been planning and preparing like we've been suggesting, there's no reason you should need to wait that long. If that sounds like you, keep reading. We'll examine the things that may be holding you back later in this chapter.

The next step is to write your launch date down. Look at it every day. Consider that date set in stone unless something truly catastrophic happens.

Now, imagine that you're waking up on that day, and everything is done. You've done everything you needed to do to prepare, and nothing has been forgotten. You're looking at everything around you—your team, your physical workspace, or even just your computer on your desk at home—and everything is exactly as it should be. All you have to do today is get to work and find some customers.

What did you do in order to make sure that happened? What were the actions that needed to be taken for you to be feeling comfortable and content (albeit, anxious in an excited way) on your launch day? Make a list of all of those things, and keep it somewhere where you will see it often. As you go through the rest of this chapter, think about how each step we list specifically applies to your business and what you need to accomplish before launch. It may be helpful to actually do each piece as you read about it.

There may be some things on our list that you hadn't thought to put on yours. Hopefully this section will cause you to think about some things you might have otherwise forgotten. That said, we encourage you to do a thorough evaluation and decide whether each piece is truly necessary before launch. We recognize that every business is different, and that what might be a requirement for one business may be able to wait a little while in another. In other words, don't panic and think you need to delay your launch date if you come across something in this section you hadn't originally listed.

Now that you have firmly set your launch date, and you have your task list in hand, it's time to start executing!

Choosing a Name

YOU MAY REMEMBER that we discussed naming your business in the first stage, and that's because thinking about names for your business is fun. It's one of the first things people start to think about when they first realize they want to start a business. If you're one of the lucky ones who came up with a great name in that first stage and haven't wavered on it all, good for you! That's one thing you can check off your list.

For most of you, the "brilliant" name idea you had in the beginning may not seem so brilliant now. A lot may have changed since you were in that first stage. You want to be sure to choose a name that accurately reflects your business and that you'll be proud of publicizing, marketing, and being associated with for the life of your business.Choosing a name for your company is a necessary jumping off point in this stage, because you will need it in order to do many of the things on your list. You'll need it to legally register your business. You'll need it to create a logo or to do any branding. You'll need it to do any marketing. You'll need it if you're opening a physical location and need signage.

A name is vital. There's no secret to choosing the "right" one, although a branding/marketing expert can help you out if you're really struggling to come up with one. Most of you probably have come up with at least a few ideas over the course of the last two stages, and it's time to pick your favorite.

Branding and Logos

Branding your company is important, and it is something that will evolve over time. Your company name is the first step towards building your brand, and it's wise to think about the general branding direction you'd like to take so that the rest of your decisions will stay in line with your big picture ideas.

First of all, let's clarify what we're talking about when we say the word "brand."

A brand encompasses so much more than just a product or a company. A brand ties together everything about a business—its products, of course, but also its company culture, its reputation in the market and with customers, its advertisements and marketing efforts, the design aesthetics of its retail locations—everything.

Think about McDonald's. You know exactly what to expect at a McDonald's in any city, in any state, across America. You instantly recognize the golden arches, and you can probably name at least five products on their menu. Whether you love them or hate them, you know them. That's what branding does. It helps people know and understand your company and what it's all about. Brands create loyalty with customers, and building a strong brand can lead you in a direction that brings you customers for life.

Branding, especially when you're a new company, is all about recognition. In this early stage, your name will be your biggest branding tool, but this is also where discussions about logos come in.

For well-established brands, logos are immediately recognizable. Apple. FedEx. Starbucks. Walmart. Google. Having a great logo that becomes synonymous with your brand is something to strive for, and many new business owners think this is a requirement. The thing is, a logo is not absolutely necessary for every business to have on launch day. Professional logo design can cost a lot of money and a lot of time. It's important to evaluate whether or not this is something your business needs right away.

Trademarking and Copyrighting

Along with naming your business and creating a recognizable brand, comes taking action to protect that name and brand. Not everyone needs to or even wants to do this, but if you're thinking about registering trademarks or copyrights, you want to start the process as soon as possible because it can take a while to become final.First of all, it's important to be clear about what copyrights and trademarks are and what they are not. A copyright pertains to creative works and publications, such as books, magazines, works of art, songs, dramatic pieces, and articles. This book, for example, is copyrighted. A trademark, on the other hand, is a legally registered symbol or word that represents or belongs to a company. Slogans like "Just Do It" are often trademarked.

Whether you decide to trademark anything about your business is entirely up to you and your vision for your company's future. The advantage of registering trademarks on slogans, logos, and names is that it grants you protection in case someone else tries to copy your materials. The disadvantage is that trademarks can be expensive to acquire, and there are a lot of nuances when it comes to registering a trademark and actually being able to present a case that holds up in court if someone uses a word, phrase, or image that belongs to your company.

For example, take Businessing Magazine, the digital publication owned by Modmacro. If the title of the magazine is trademarked, Modmacro could probably successfully litigate against another company if they tried to create a magazine with the exact same name. The word "businessing" by itself, however? Probably not. If Modmacro registered a trademark on that word, it may discourage other companies from trying to use it, but they may not be able to bring a suit against someone if they did. It's much more difficult to secure exclusivity on single words out of context like that.

Trademarking issues are best handled by an attorney. They have experience with trademark suits and know what can be protected and what has the best chance of being granted exclusivity that can be defended in court.

A quick note about attorneys: Even those of you who aren't considering registering trademarks should start building a relationship with an attorney. There are lots of issues that come up in the early stages of a business that require the attention of an attorney. In the next part of this section, we'll go into more detail about legal concerns and why you should be consulting with an attorney sooner rather than later.

╫ Matt: When it comes to creating a logo, you have to either do it all the way or don't do it at all. The problem is that people can get initially scared off by the price, and then they end up cutting corners. They find out that a professional logo design is going to cost somewhere between $1,500 and $3,000, and they decide that they don't want to spend that kind of money up front. They hear that their buddy's cousin will design a logo for $84.95, and they do that instead.

From my experience in branding and marketing, I strongly advise against that. If it's about the money, it's better to not have a logo at all in the beginning than to have an amateur design that doesn't fit with your brand and that you're going to end up changing anyway. In some industries, the whole logo discussion is really a distraction in disguise, because you don't need one. Real estate agents are an example of this. Most of them never need a logo during their entire career. They just use a headshot and the logo of whatever broker they're working under.

In other industries, a logo is necessary. If your industry demands that you have professional marketing materials or vehicle graphics—those kinds of things require professional logos. In those types of industries, you need to spend the money on a good design. You may have to get creative in order to come up with the money to do it, but it will be worth it.

I recognize this is more difficult if you don't have a preexisting relationship with a graphic designer, but this is the stage where you need to start building those kinds of relationships anyway. It's a little bit more work to start calling people, but it's better to do it sooner rather than later. If you're not sure where to start, I'd encourage you to take a look at what we do at Modmacro. We'd love to take some time with you and see if we can help with what you need. If not, we can at least be an initial contact to point you in the right direction.

╫ Jessica: In publishing, books need to have their publishing imprint logo on them, so for us, getting a logo was a high priority. However, the truth is that we didn't really need to have that logo in order to launch. We just needed it before publishing any books. Sure, we wanted it on our website, and we wanted to use it for branding purposes, but it wasn't absolutely necessary for launch.

We were lucky in that we already had a relationship with a graphic designer. We knew exactly who would be designing our logo, and it was easy to reach out to him and get it done. If we hadn't had that relationship in place, it probably could have waited.

You'll hear us say this a lot throughout this chapter, but we stand by it wholeheartedly, so we don't mind repeating ourselves a bit: If it's not absolutely necessary, don't delay your launch over it. Keep it on the list, but make it a priority when you need to and not before. Things like logo design can very easily become excuses not to launch on time.

Forming a Legal Entity

THIS MAY BE one of the more tedious aspects of starting a business, but it is vital. In order to comply with tax rules and regulations, you likely need to register your business with your state's governing agency. Doing this requires that you decide what legal structure your business will have, and that choice can determine how much your business pays in taxes and how well it separates your personal assets from liability if something happens to your business. It's an important decision to make, and while you can change it later if the nature of your business changes, you don't want to do that unless you have to. Changing your business entity is a much more involved process than initially setting it up.

Some of you may be thinking, "my business is so small, I don't need to go through any legal hoops. That's a waste of time and money and far too complicated for what I'm trying to do." If you are monetizing a hobby and have zero intention of growing, you might be able to make that argument. Just know that you are taking a risk, and when tax time comes, you may be more likely to be audited, because income coming from a non-registered business is a red flag. The time and trouble it takes to go through an IRS audit is far more frustrating than the time it takes to register your business and create a proper legal structure.

If you truly are trying to create a company, you need to form a legal entity of some kind. There's no way around it. Fortunately, there are a variety of options. For example, if you are working alone, you can create a sole proprietorship, which is a very simple and inexpensive process. Most states don't even require registration for sole proprietorships, only that you either use your own name for the business or file a "doing business as" (DBA) name. Sole proprietorships are how many businesses start out, and then as they grow, they may end up incorporating.

If there are others on your team who will own a percentage of the company, you can register as a partnership, a limited liability corporation (LLC), or you can fully incorporate by forming an S-Corp or a C-Corp. Each type of entity has advantages and drawbacks, and you'll have to evaluate what will work best for you. The simpler the structure, the easier it is upfront, and the less expensive it is. Simpler structures require far less paperwork, and there are fewer regulations. The downside is that personal liability is higher. On the other hand, corporate structures require more work to set up, but they are more protective in the long run, especially if you intend to grow or eventually sell your company.

The actual process of registering your business is not terribly time-consuming, and you can do it online in most states. Different states have different tax laws, some of which are friendlier than others, and you may decide that registering your business in a state other than your own is the best choice for tax purposes. If your physical location is not an integral part of your business (if you are conducting all of your business online, for example), then this can be a wise choice. It does require an extra step; you must have a physical address in whatever state you register in, and there must be a designated person (called a registered agent) who can be responsible for your business in that state. If you don't personally know someone who can do this for you, there are companies dedicated to maintaining physical addresses and registered agents for out-of-state business owners.

This all may sound like a lot, but it really isn't that difficult. You just need to get it done. In order to do some of the other things on your list (create bank accounts, sign contracts, etc.), you will need to have your legal entity established. Once you have chosen a name for your business, go ahead and take the time to get it registered. It will make everything else much, much easier.

Working with an Attorney

At this stage, you may be wondering why you would need an attorney. In a perfect world, attorneys are not necessary unless something has gone wrong. In the business world, it's a little more complicated than that. Attorneys are useful and downright necessary in all kinds of scenarios, even ones that don't directly involve litigation.

If your business requires you to provide contracts to clients, you'll want an attorney to write that contract and make sure that it is legally sound. If you need to trademark any piece of your name, your product, or your marketing materials, you'll want an attorney to help you navigate that process. If you are applying for patents, an attorney can make sure you present the strongest case possible. If the structure of your company is at all complicated, you'll want an attorney to help you with your operating agreement to ensure that everyone who has a stake in the business is treated fairly.

Attorneys, like insurance, are best obtained before they're needed. Sometimes, situations or opportunities arise suddenly, and it's much better to have an established relationship with an attorney so you can make a phone call and handle it.

You do not want to be in a situation where you are faced with something (good or bad) and have no one to turn to for legal advice. Building a relationship at that point costs you valuable time, and you may find that you don't get a favorable outcome because you couldn't act quickly enough.

It's tough. New business owners love coming up with company names and ideas for logos. They like thinking about product design ideas and taglines for their marketing materials. These things don't cost money to do, and the time they cost is enjoyable. Entrepreneurs generally love the creative aspects of the job. What they don't love is going out and building relationships with attorneys, accountants, bankers, etc. That part takes time and effort, and it can be frustrating. Some people are lucky, and they already have a friend or cousin or brother-in-law who is an attorney. Most of us aren't that lucky and need to invest time into finding someone and building the relationship from the ground up.

The best advice we can give is to do it as soon as possible, preferably long before you think you need to. When it comes time for you to call on an attorney's services, you'll be so glad you could just make a quick phone call and be done.

⸬ Matt: In thinking about why you should build a relationship with an attorney as early as possible, I go back to the trademarking conversation. If you have a decent attorney, you can probably get a national trademark for around $1500, which in the grand scheme of things is not that much. Most people end up not doing it, though, because they don't have a relationship with an attorney, and they don't want to go out and build one.

So, if you'd started a relationship with that attorney before you launched, then you could have just called and made it happen when you needed to.

I used to think the thing that stopped most new business owners from relying on professionals like attorneys and accountants was money. I've found that in some cases that's true, but more often, they just don't want to call people and find someone. It's too much work. If someone had walked up to them and said, "Give me $200 right now and I'll go find you a great attorney," they probably would have done it because the money is easier to spend than the time and frustration of finding someone.

Of course it's frustrating. You have to take the time to network or get referrals from friends and follow up, and there's no guarantee the referrals you get will even work out. You could end up finding someone who came highly recommended from a friend, but by the time you finally get in their office (which could be weeks later), you find out you don't want to work with that person after all. Then you have to start all over again.

You'll think, "I'll just wait until I really need them," because you don't want to spend two more weeks of your time.

Here's the thing. Do it anyway. All the experience you gain in finding that person, and then all the experience you gain in working with them (even if you don't like them) is valuable experience you can take to the next relationship. The process, as frustrating as it can be, will be instrumental in helping you find someone you do like and that you can work with for a long, long time.

✝ Jessica: From the very beginning of Maven, we had a long-term vision, and while our initial structure was simple, we knew it was going to get complicated relatively quickly. We realized early that we were going to need to consult with a few professionals to make sure we set everything up correctly. Finding both an attorney and an accountant was a high priority.

I'm glad we did this, because we've had several situations come up, and it's been such a relief to just pick up the phone and have someone on hand to help us out. Now, anytime we need anything—a contract drawn up, a tricky negotiation of book rights, or something as mundane as annual taxes, we're set.

The process of finding the right people wasn't easy, though. It took several weeks in order to find someone who would even return my phone call. There were multiple times where I thought, "We can do this ourselves. We don't really need these people right now. Maybe we can just wait until it's more urgent." I worried that I might be wasting time that could've been better spent doing something else for the business.

I just had to remind myself that it would be better to spend the time at the beginning, while things hadn't gotten too busy yet, rather than have to scramble later, when we were already juggling other, more complicated issues.

Opening Bank Accounts

BEFORE YOU START collecting any revenue, you're going to need a place for that revenue to go. A designated bank account is absolutely necessary for your business. Yet, this is one of those things that doesn't seem all that urgent. You don't need a bank account until you have launched and you're taking money from customers, right? Not so fast.

One of the things we've tried to communicate clearly is that some tasks in this stage are best left to professionals. Can you imagine hiring a graphic designer to work on a logo for your business, only to realize after the work is done that you don't have a way to pay them? Sure, you can pay out of your personal account if it comes down to that, but it's so much more streamlined to pay for a business expense out of a designated business account.

For those of you who are running a sole proprietorship, setting up a bank account for your business is simple. You can create a new account that is essentially an additional personal account. The time and paperwork involved is minimal, and it's as easy to manage as your current personal account.

If you're building a partnership or corporation, it's a little more complicated, but it is far better to take the extra time to do it correctly from the beginning than to try and cut corners, only to go through a frustrating process later. Opening an official business account with a bank will require you to have all of your business's legal information on hand. You'll need your incorporation documents and your Employer Identification Number (EIN). You'll also need some personal information about the other business owners. It takes a few hours to sit with a banker and go through the whole process, but once it's done, it's done. You can now use that account for all of your business expenses.

What you absolutely cannot do is comingle your funds with your personal account. This will become a nightmare very quickly. At best, comingling is confusing, and it can cause awkward situations and poor decision-making. It's much harder to instantly assess the financial state of your business and to accurately "know your numbers" when you aren't keeping separate records and separate accounts. At the worst, you may find yourself facing tax penalties or legal difficulties if a major event like divorce or bankruptcy comes up.

╫ Matt: I started as a sole proprietor, so I started by opening a "business account," which was really just another personal account that was designated as the bank account for the business. Because I was working alone, I didn't need to have any special designations for the account—the only requirement was that it needed to be separate from my family's finances.

Once Modmacro got to the point where we were bigger and needed to incorporate, I needed to close that account and open multiple official business accounts. That was the natural evolution of the company, and there's nothing wrong with doing it that way if you're starting as a one-man band. If you have no immediate need to incorporate, that is the simplest way to get started.

As we've said, what's not okay is comingling funds. I have worked with clients who have said things like "I had money to pay you for your work on our website, but then my wife went and bought something." My first thought is always that they're referring to a business purchase, which is bad money management, but at least makes sense. Unfortunately, they usually respond by telling me they've mixed up their household and business funds, and now they're in a bind.

Running your finances that way will cause you degrees of both business and personal trouble that you'd be wise to avoid.

╫ Jessica: Setting up our company's bank account was almost an afterthought. We were about to get paid for a job and very suddenly realized we didn't have a proper place for that money to go. We needed a bank account and we needed it quickly. The problem was: we hadn't gotten our legal structure in place yet.

Thinking it would be easy to adjust later, I did exactly what Matt did. I set up another personal account that I set aside for anything and everything to do with Maven. This would have been fine for someone who is working alone, but I'm not. I have a partner.

After a little time had passed and we were getting into more complicated jobs, we realized that we both needed access to the bank account. We'd had our legal structure in place for a while by that point, so the solution was obvious: Go to the bank with all of our business documentation, and have them change the account to reflect our partnership.

It was so much more difficult than I ever could have imagined. The original banker who set up my additional personal account assured me that it would be an easy transition if I just brought in all of our partnership documents. It was not. Not only did I end up needing to take multiple trips to the bank, but the whole thing also confused our accountant to the point where I think he seriously considered dropping us as a client. It ended up being unnecessarily complicated.

Here's what we should have done: We should have gotten our legal structure figured out right away so that I had all of our documentation on hand. Then, I should have gone straight to the bank and set the accounts up correctly the first time, long before we ever needed them. We were in a hurry, and it clouded our judgment. Cutting corners ended up costing us valuable time in the end.

Manufacturing Your Products

FOR SOME OF you, this section may not apply. If you are starting a service-based business, manufacturing may not be a concern. On the other hand, for those of you who will be selling products, manufacturing is critical. You need to know how and where your products will be manufactured, as well as how much it will cost and how long the process will take.

In the previous stage, you hopefully started researching manufacturing options. Now, it's time to make some decisions so you can get the manufacturing process started, work out any kinks, and have enough product on hand for your launch day.

Choosing the Right Manufacturer

When it comes to manufacturing, you are looking for the right balance between quality and cost. That may seem obvious, but it's all too easy to fall into the trap of choosing the cheapest option without considering what you may be compromising in quality. Money is such an immediate and pressing concern for many startups; it's important to remember that it cannot guide *all* of your decisions.

Manufacturing is an enormous global industry, and some parts of the world are known for manufacturing certain products. For example, South Korea has become a world leader in electronics manufacturing, so for tech startups, Korea may be a good place to begin your search. China often comes to mind as a top manufacturing destination for many industries, but other countries like Vietnam and Malaysia are building more and more factories as well. Just keep in mind that it's also well understood that many overseas manufacturers deliver much lower quality standards.

On the other hand, you may decide that domestic manufacturing is important to your business's values, and depending on the industry, that may be a reasonable option. By keeping your manufacturing process close to home, you'll likely be able to visit the factory more often, and language barriers won't be a concern-where they might be at an overseas factory. The "Made in the USA" label also comes with a high perceived value, which could set your business apart from the competition. The biggest downside to domestic manufacturing is usually the cost, which is typically significantly higher than manufacturing abroad, but the quality is typically much higher as well, thus playing into the value equation.

One of the most important things to do when deciding on a manufacturer is to personally visit the facility. Referrals from friends and colleagues can be helpful, as can websites and photos, but the only way to truly evaluate a manufacturer is to go there yourself and speak with the people you'd be working with on a regular basis. By being on-site, you will be able to observe their attention to detail and quality, and you will see what it's like to communicate and partner with the company's leaders.

And that's just it. A manufacturer truly needs to feel like a partner to your business. They are the ones trusted with the task of making your products, so they need to have similar values, and they need to be as invested in your company's success as you are.

Hiring an Expert

If the very idea of finding a manufacturer for your product seems overwhelming, you're not alone. Lots of new business owners are overwhelmed by all the different factors to consider, not to mention all of the other tasks you're already working on to prepare to launch your business.

Even an experienced entrepreneur like Daymond John, founder and CEO of clothing giant FUBU, didn't feel confident about his knowledge in manufacturing when he first launched his company. He says that he knew "how to sew, but that's different than manufacturing. Sewing is an ability; manufacturing is a knowledge... For example, you need the knowledge of how to interpret your designs for overseas, how to be cost effective, how much embroidery machines may cost per hour to run, how much it costs to ship the product back to the States, etc."

He was fortunate to have someone on his team who studied at the Fashion Institute of Technology and who had some experience working with different clothing manufacturers. He knew it would have been difficult for him to acquire that knowledge himself, and that it was much better for him to rely on his partner in the early days rather than take time away from his area of expertise, which is marketing, to learn the ins and outs of manufacturing.If you don't already have someone on your team with experience in the manufacturing industry, you may be better off hiring someone to do your search for you. There are agents who specialize in sourcing and manufacturing, and they can help you by visiting factories, building relationships, and conducting thorough cost-benefit analyses on your behalf. Just like we tell you to hire experts for specialized things like legal issues and accounting, manufacturing is an area where you may benefit from freeing up your time and allowing someone with much more knowledge and experience than yourself to take the helm.

Marketing Your Company

W E'RE GOING TO go out on a limb here and say that marketing is probably not something most entrepreneurs are thinking about at this stage. Most of you are busy getting all of your ducks in a row, thinking you will begin your marketing efforts once you've launched. For some of you, that may be a completely reasonable strategy. If you already have a network of people you're working with that you're going to be able to engage with as soon as you launch, then you probably don't need to start marketing heavily ahead of time. You'll get a few customers right away from your own contacts, and then the snowball effect may take hold.

For many of you, though, you shouldn't wait until you've already launched to start getting customers in the door. You want the customers to be lining up, waiting for you, rather than the other way around. This is why it makes sense to start your marketing efforts well ahead of your launch date.

There are a lot of pieces to the marketing puzzle, but one of the most basic and obvious ones is a website. These days, people often think of social media first, but a website that you own is a much more powerful marketing tool. You control it, and it's yours for life. You don't have to worry about an outside company like Facebook or Google suddenly changing their policies, forcing you to start from scratch. We have heard horror stories about businesses depending on social media and then losing hundreds of customer reviews due to a server change or a new platform being introduced. Don't let that happen to you; invest in building a website.

If you are lucky enough to have someone on your team who has a professional background in marketing and web design, you may be able to take care of this task in-house, but most of you will probably need to look outside your immediate circle for someone to handle this for you. Like logo design, this is not an area where you want to skimp on quality just to save a few dollars. The upfront savings is not worth the trouble it will cause you down the road when you realize that you want your whole site redesigned. It is far better to invest the money now and get it done right the first time. Remember, your website may be the first impression anyone has of you.

The other thing to keep in mind when building a website, whether it's being done by someone on your team or an outside professional, is that it takes time. A professional website often takes 90 days from concept to completion, and that's if everything goes smoothly. Do not wait until a week before your launch date to contact a web design professional. Jump on this task sooner rather than later so that it's ready to go by the time you launch. If you are able to get it done early, you may even be able to use it to build a following before your official launch.

Besides ensuring that you have a website up and running, there are other marketing efforts you may want to get up and rolling well before you launch. After all, if you only begin marketing after you've launched, you're starting off at a disadvantage.

Depending on your industry, some marketing channels may be more effective than others. For some businesses, a strong social media presence can be very helpful. For others, efforts may be better spent drumming up excitement in the local area and reaching out to people in the community directly.

In this stage, you have a lot going on. You want to be efficient and use your time wisely. Marketing is extremely important, but it can quickly become a time sink if you are not doing it in a targeted way. If you are unsure as to where to focus your marketing budget, consult a professional or a colleague in your industry. If you have no past marketing experience, you'll benefit immensely from someone who either specializes in it or someone who knows your industry well enough to know what works and what doesn't.

The main point here is that the earlier you begin to think about marketing, the better. Waiting until launch only makes sense if you already have a solid plan for getting customers in right away. Your business will not survive without customers, and letting them know who you are and what you do is the only way to bring them in.

✚ Matt: Marketing is an umbrella term that we use to include digital marketing, direct marketing, advertising, Search Engine Optimization (SEO), public relations, social media, and much more. We always recommend starting with your website. First, your business is expected to have a website, and it needs to be professional, welcoming, and informative. During the website design process, you'll be forced to consider important components that will be useful for all other marketing you'll do.

For example, branding elements need to be established, content and strategic messaging comes into play, and being able to identify and communicate your target audience is a must. At Modmacro, we often assist startups with both planning and executing all of these things. Most of our clients don't walk in the door with each of these pieces in place and fully fleshed out.

Any opportunity you uncover that attracts the attention of your target audience, wherever they hang out either on- or offline, is gold. For some clients, it's easier to plan. They don't necessarily have the confidence right off the bat to execute those plans.

I remember working with a client a few years back who wanted to print business cards so that he would have something to give out at an upcoming promotional event. He was frantic because the event was taking place the following day, and he didn't have his cards printed yet. Why not? Because his company didn't have a logo.

My suggestion to him was to drop everything he was doing, head to a local print shop, and have some clean, simple, professional business cards made up. Business cards don't always have logos, and not everyone thinks twice about that. If a business card has all of the relevant contact information on it, that's at least a great start, and better than walking in empty-handed

In this scenario, what would you do? If you'd rather miss a promotional event that could be a tremendous marketing opportunity for your brand new business than give out logo-less business cards, then you will struggle up to, and probably after, launch day. Instead, find a reasonable solution, and don't let a great opportunity pass you by.

Being a business owner requires a lot of confidence, and sometimes you have to create that confidence. Waiting for a logo, waiting for a website, waiting for any number of things can be an excuse, and you have to resist that urge. If you have a networking event tomorrow, it makes no sense to skip the event in favor of waiting three weeks for professional logo design.

✟ Jessica: Marketing is a tricky thing with a business like Maven because our product is highly specialized and caters to a specific niche of people. Mass, untargeted marketing would be mostly ineffective for us, so we didn't put much effort into pre-launch publicity. We had a few well-established relationships and a few jobs lined up as we were getting started, and we felt like our energy would be best spent nurturing the relationships we already had.

I still think this was a wise decision. We were extremely busy in those early days, and mindlessly throwing a bunch of time and money into marketing would have been a distraction from other critical actions. We knew we would need to do some marketing eventually, but we also knew that it would require planning and strategy in order for it to be meaningful.

That said, the word "busy" can sometimes just be a substitute word for "stalling" or "scared," and we have to be careful with that in everything we do. Our situation was a little different in that one of the things keeping us busy was a handful of actual client projects, but it's very easy to throw the word "busy" around and to use it as an excuse.

Like most things, whether or not to do a bunch of marketing before launch is up to you and the nature of your business, but I agree with Matt in that people need to find out about your business somehow. It's important to have some kind of plan in place, even if that means you'll be taking a slower and more methodical approach to marketing.

Obtaining Licenses, Permits, and Certifications

FOR CERTAIN BUSINESSES, licenses and/or permits are a must. For example, a restaurant that will have alcoholic beverages on the menu needs to obtain a liquor license before opening. A food truck needs to obtain operating permits, and must submit to rigorous inspections. If your business requires the construction of a new building or even the renovation of an existing space, there are permits needed for that, too.

Applying for licenses and permits can be a time-consuming and painstaking process. Different states and even different cities have different requirements for what is and is not allowed, and it sometimes requires a lot of extra labor in order to get a space "up to code."

This can become a frustrating experience, and it is wise to give yourself way more time than you think you'll need. A well-known café in San Francisco, California had built two booming locations on opposite sides of the city, and they were hoping to expand across the bay into Oakland by opening a third location. They chose the location and started renovating the space to accommodate their own needs, plus they needed to make some alterations in order to comply with zoning and city codes. Their opening date was set for April 1, 2015.

By the end of February, the renovations were done, but the owner needed final approval from the city inspector before she could begin moving in all of the equipment and putting final touches on the décor. By the time the inspector finally made it out to the café, it was mid-March, and he determined that the floor that had been installed was too slippery and therefore unsafe for an establishment that would be serving beverages.

The owner was frustrated and knew that the original opening date wouldn't be possible. She'd given herself the time she thought she needed based on the other two locations she'd opened, but with this location being in a different city, she hadn't realized she would need two or three extra months. She didn't expect any surprises in dealing with city officials.

Finally, after several more inspections and a near-refusal from the city to issue the business a permit at all after all the problems they were having, the café opened in August.

Start applying for permits and licenses early, and expect that the process will take weeks, and maybe months longer than you think it will. It is much better to allow yourself some extra time up front than to find yourself in a situation where you have to delay your announced opening.

Certifications

Certifications in most industries are less cut-and-dry than licenses and permits. Licenses and permits are required for legal reasons, and you cannot open your doors without them. Certifications may be required for legal reasons, but often aren't. They show that you've completed a certain amount of training or education in an area, and you will have to decide whether they are important for you or for any of your staff members.

For example, in the cyber security industry, there are dozens upon dozens of different certifications, all with specific applications. If you're in that field and looking for a job at a large company, then collecting as many specialized certifications as possible can help set you apart among a large sea of applicants.

On the other hand, if you're trying to start your own cyber security firm, you don't need to worry about standing out from other applicants. You need to worry about attracting customers and gaining their trust in your experience. Depending on your target audience, they may not know the different certifications available and what they all mean. Security+ and CISSP are considered to be two of the most marketable certifications to have in the industry, but is it worth delaying your opening by months or even years to ensure that everyone on your staff has both? Probably not.

Do your research and find out what's industry-standard. Even then, you may not need to have them completed by the time you open your doors for business. If you can still find customers and complete jobs while you're working towards getting some of the elite certifications that will keep you competitive in your industry, then that is ideal. You will build customer loyalty based on your work, not based on pieces of paper hanging on your wall.

✝ Matt: We've worked with several small businesses over the years that aren't required to earn any certifications to operate. Often, there isn't a legal requirement or even an industry standard. But some startups get fixated on the fact that the top companies in their industry hold certain certifications, and they're not willing to launch until they have them as well.

I understand that thinking, and in some cases it may be important to launch with those certifications in place to be competitive. But that's not usually the case. Consider how long earning those certifications will delay your launch. Anything that slows you down needs to be well worth it. That's why some business owners don't even worry about certifications until they're in business for five or ten years. I'm actually working with a client right now who just told me that she's delaying building her website and launching her business because she wants to get a number of certifications first. After researching her industry, I found that a lot of people aren't even getting those certifications in their entire 30-year careers.

She believes that the certifications will help set her apart, and they will. But she'll have to launch six months to a year later than she wants to. To me, it seems like she'll be past the point of diminishing return.

If a permit or certification is a legal issue or a basic industry standard, then you should make it a priority. If it's not an absolute requirement, then it probably makes more sense to launch first and start bringing in customers. Meanwhile, you can start building relationships with the organizations that issue the certifications. This way, you can begin to build your brand and establish client relationships right away, and you can work toward earning those certifications when it makes sense. Life is short, and delaying your launch unnecessarily may be something you'll regret later on. I know I would.

✝ Jessica: Certifications are not a huge deal in the publishing industry, and we're lucky that we didn't have to worry about permits or licenses either. I can see, though, how all of these things can end up being a roadblock in getting your business off the ground.

The bureaucratic roadblock presented by licenses and permits can only be mitigated by giving yourself a lot of extra time and by planning ahead. I think with those kinds of things, you almost have to expect that something will go wrong, and plan for worse than the worst-case scenario.

With certifications, I can see those being a confidence-builder, but like Matt, I do think you have to be careful with anything that's going to delay your launch. Get your business started, sell some jobs or products, and let that be your confidence. You'll have time to get certifications later.

Final Thoughts About Stage Three

Things are really coming together now, and you are well on your way to launching your business.

In fact, if you've followed the advice in this chapter, you have already set a launch date. Maybe you've gotten all of your planning done early, and now you have a few extra weeks to double- and triple-check everything. Maybe you're down to the wire and your proposed launch date is six hours from now.

Whether you've got a big window of time ahead of you, or hardly any window at all, you should have completed all of the tasks that are *absolutely necessary* for you to start taking customers. This doesn't mean that you'll *feel* ready to launch—most business owners have that nagging feeling that things aren't quite perfect, and that is perfectly normal. As long as all of the absolutely necessary tasks are complete, you can launch, even if you don't feel ready. If there are things you forgot to take care of, or even things you skipped on purpose, you can always get them done once you've started bringing in customers and making some money.

So get launched already! Open your doors! Put your website up! Let everyone know that your company is open for business.

Stage Four:
Launch

.

Launch Day Is Only the Beginning

THIS IS THE day you've been working up to. This day is so important, because it is the first day of your new venture. This is when you see all of your planning pay off, and you see your dreams of becoming a business owner turn into reality.

Hopefully all of that sounds good to you. It should. Launch day is an exciting time. Make sure you do something celebratory to reward yourself for all of the work you've put in up to this point, even if it's just something small or symbolic.

Then, it's time to get right back to work, because this last stage includes much more than just launch day. Those first few weeks and months are critical for your new business, and you need to be as vigilant and dedicated as ever. How many times have you seen a new restaurant or store open in your local area, only to close within a year? It happens all the time. Business owners so often fall into the trap of thinking customers will magically start pouring in on day one, and that mentality ends up being their downfall.

So as you go through the first days, weeks, and months of being a business owner, here are some questions to ask yourself, and some things to consider.

Where Are the Customers?

THAT FIRST DAY is interesting. You've spent all this time planning and preparing to start your business; it's probably the only thing you've had on your mind lately. If you followed the advice in the previous sections of this book, you've been talking about your business and doing some marketing. With that in mind, you may be expecting customers to flow in right away. If you're one of the fortunate ones, you may even have some definite jobs lined up so that you hit the ground running.

Most of you, however, even if you've done your due diligence in spreading the word (and even if you're working with a professional marketing firm), will not have customers rushing in on your first day. It takes time to build buzz and draw attention to your business, which is why we recommend getting such an early start. If you haven't, and you're realizing now on launch day that customers will not magically find you, you have a challenge ahead of you.

Finding customers is the biggest challenge most new business owners face, so this needs to be priority number one. It's easy to sit back and think that customers will show up eventually, but if you don't take action, they may not show up at all—at least not at the rate you need in order to stay in business.

Look at Your Immediate Network

The first place to go looking for customers is in your own immediate network of friends and family. This is not to say that everyone in your family and all of your friends will become customers themselves, but they need to know that your business is up and running, and they need to know that you're looking for customers. You never know who might be in their networks.

A tip to increase your chances of success is to be specific about what you're looking for. It's probably not enough to tell your friends during a night out that you've got a new business. They'll be excited that you have a new venture in your life, and they'll be supportive, but they may not think to tell others. What's more effective is to say, "I just launched my business, and we're looking to grow it. If you know any people who would benefit from what we're doing, tell them about me." The more specific you can be, the better.

Self-promotion feels weird at first, especially if you're not used to it. You have to do it anyway. Word of mouth is the cheapest form of marketing that exists, and it also happens to be the most effective. Building word of mouth starts with people who already know you and who trust that you're a reliable person who would do good work.

Any circle you belong to, whether that's a church, a book club, a networking group, or even just a group of friends that gets together every weekend to watch football—is the potential start of a web of contacts that can reach much farther than you can on your own. Your friend's cousin may have never met you, but if your friend explains to his cousin what your business is all about and how it can solve a particular problem his cousin has, then that is probably enough to get you a face-to-face meeting. That lead didn't cost you a penny and could turn into a paying job.

If you aren't in any social or professional circles, or if you are having trouble turning your immediate connections into leads, it's time to look into making some new connections that could be beneficial. A great place to start is with networking groups in your industry. If you're near a large metropolitan area, there's a good chance you'll find a group related to your industry that meets regularly, and you can go introduce yourself in person. If you're in a smaller town, or in a more obscure industry, you may not find a convenient in-person meeting. Fortunately, the internet is a great resource for various professional forums and places to connect. LinkedIn is usually a good place to start, and Google searches can be helpful, too.

Leverage the Customers You Do Have

Once you do get some leads, even if it's only a few at first, it's important to build on those leads. Anyone who experiences your business as a customer is a great resource to anyone else who might be thinking about becoming one. Think about your own behavior as a customer. When you're looking for a new restaurant, or when you're thinking about ordering a product online, do you look at reviews before jumping in? Nowadays, most people do. Positive reviews from early customers can do wonders for your reputation.

There are different ways to go about encouraging your customers to share their opinions of your business. The most obvious and least intrusive way to do so is to do outstanding work. Take care of your customers and provide them with a memorable experience. Customers who have a positive experience with you or with your business will talk to a friend or two about it. Of course the flip side of this is true, too. Customers who have a bad experience will probably talk to ten of their friends, so be careful not to let anyone fall through the cracks.

Depending on your industry, it may even be acceptable to ask your customers to leave reviews. In the publishing industry, book reviews are golden, and it's normal to have a page at the end of the book that asks the reader to leave a review. Readers have come to expect this, especially from e-books. I have also seen restaurants and other customer service-oriented businesses (salons, spas, tattoo shops, etc.) specifically ask their clients to leave reviews on Yelp, Facebook, and Google+.

Another way your customers can help you is by giving testimonials. Testimonials are similar to reviews in that they give the customer an opportunity to share their experience, but a testimonial is entirely positive. Businesses usually share testimonials on their websites, and sometimes in their marketing materials. If you truly go above and beyond for a customer, they may send you a testimonial without you asking for one. That's always a great surprise, and the only way for that to happen is for you to blow a customer's mind. It's also okay to ask for testimonials, especially from customers you have a good relationship with.

Some business owners, especially in the beginning, offer to do free work for friends or family in exchange for testimonials. If used wisely and sparingly, this can be a really powerful thing. If you do an amazing job for those people, and they provide you with a meaningful testimonial, then that can help you build your reputation right from the start. You have to be a little careful, though, because you want to limit your free work. You don't want word spreading to your friend's friends and then out to their friends that you're offering up free work for everyone.

Finally, some businesses offer incentives to customers who give referrals. This is common practice for a wide variety of businesses, such as dentist offices, chiropractic practices, and many subscription-based services like gyms and health clubs. For some businesses, this works well and brings in a steady flow of new customers. Just know that this can get tricky, because anytime you're offering a discount or incentive, you're opening the door to diminish the perceived value of your product or service. We'll get into more detail about discounts later in this chapter.

Marketing, Marketing, Marketing

We've discussed marketing in previous chapters, because we believe it's imperative to start thinking about it early in the process. Marketing takes time to become effective, and the more lead-time you give yourself before launching, the better. If you have seen your early marketing efforts pay off and you have some customers right away when you launch, congratulations! That's the ideal scenario. If you haven't seen any results yet, that's okay, just don't quit. In fact, since you've launched now, you would be wise to look at the kind of marketing you're doing, and analyze whether or not it's effective. You may find that you need to step up your current efforts, or you may even need to change course altogether.

Tapping into your immediate circle of contacts and leveraging your current customers is vital to creating buzz and word-of-mouth referrals. However, alone, it's not enough. Without marketing you simply will not be visible to enough people to sustain you. You may survive on immediate contacts for a few months, but what if it takes another four months for a new customer to come in? Most people would be out of business in that time.

Marketing scares a lot of people because they think it's complicated, or because they think it won't work. People worry about spending money on it, especially if it doesn't produce immediate meaningful results. This is why we recommend working with a professional. Marketing professionals understand what will and will not work in various industries, and they can help you spend your dollars wisely. They can help you create coherent messaging, and they can help you get it out to the right people. They can keep you from wasting time and money on things that aren't likely to bring customers to you.

Then there are people who are hesitant to try any marketing because they've had a bad experience. For example, the owner of an ammunition store in San Diego realized that his business was already struggling after only being open for four or five months. He ran a newspaper ad when the store first opened, but didn't see any traffic from it. He then tried hiring someone to hold a sign out in front of the store for a few weeks, but again, didn't see any results. After those experiences, he was hesitant to spend any more money on marketing in case it didn't pan out.

His story has a happy ending though. A few of his competitors ended up closing their doors, and being the last man standing gave him an advantage. Plus, he had finally decided to do some work with a professional marketing firm, and that helped him survive while the businesses around him were going under. Now he's able to rely mostly on word-of-mouth, and he hardly spends any of his budget on marketing. While it's great for him that his business is thriving now, his story could have turned out much differently if he hadn't given marketing another try.

The other lesson to learn from this storeowner is that he could find himself in the same situation in the future if he's not careful. Sure, he's not spending much money on marketing right now, which is a good thing for his budget, but it has taken him several years to get to this point. Plus, relying on word-of-mouth alone is very risky. He doesn't have control over what people say about his business, and that is a scary prospect.

Marketing is necessary. It's telling people who you are and what your business is about. Your friends and family will get you to a certain point, and your current customers will get you a step beyond that, but if you really want to keep a steady flow of customers, you need to let the world know your business exists.

‡ Matt: When I started my business, I got the word out to my immediate network as soon as I could. I talked about my business a lot, especially with my friends at my church. I learned very quickly, however, that saying, "I started a website company, tell everyone you know" was ineffective. What was much more effective was telling everyone "Here's the type of work I do, and here is the type of people I'm looking for as clients. If you have a friend or colleague who is that type of person, please tell them about me."

At church, everyone knew I was working with small, typically service-oriented businesses, and everyone was on the lookout for friends or friends-of-friends who were starting companies and needed websites. Because I was being specific and clearly articulating who I was looking for, I actually got a lot of great initial leads through church. They weren't huge projects, but they were enough for me to get my company off the ground, and many of those leads ended up pointing me towards bigger and bigger jobs.

‡ Jessica: I'll admit that I struggled with this at first. It's not easy for me to promote myself, and it felt strange to transition from saying, "I'm a writer" to saying, "I just started a company." The difference in response has been incredible, though. When I would talk about being a writer, people would tell me their vague thoughts about writing a book someday, or they would say things like, "Wow, I always wondered if I could write for a living." They were nice conversations, and I'll talk to anyone about writing for hours, but it wasn't helpful for the business.

Now, when I tell friends or even people I'm meeting for the first time about Maven and the kinds of books we publish, almost every single person says, "I know someone who is thinking about writing a book for their business. They just weren't sure how to do it." I give them my contact information to pass on, and if their friend turns out to be serious about needing a book to help position and market their business, then they have a person to call.

The leads don't always pan out, but that's not really the point. I'm just happy to have people talking about Maven and spreading the idea that books can be phenomenal marketing tools for business owners. Getting the word out is the first step.

How Is the Business Doing?

THE EARLY DAYS of any business are crucial. This is when you're building your reputation, and you're trying to survive in a volatile world. Even if you're fortunate enough to have a steady flow of customers from the start, there is no guarantee that it will keep going. You have to constantly be proactive, and you have to constantly be making decisions and taking actions that will propel your business forward. In order to make those decisions, you need to be evaluating everything in your business all the time.

It's easy to get complacent, especially when things seem to be going well. If customers are pouring in and the business is making money, it's tempting to sit back, relax, and not ask yourself any hard questions. The truth is, even if everything is going well, there is always room for improvement. Only by breaking down each day and each process, will you be able to analyze whether or not you're doing things in the most efficient and effective way possible.

The best way to analyze your progress is with specific measurements. It's not enough to say things "feel" like they're going well, or that it "seems" like a particular product is selling better than another. You have to look at actual data to know for sure. Concrete numbers are much more helpful for guiding business decisions than guesses or assumptions.

Inventory Selection

If your business sells products, this means looking at each SKU and tracking your sales numbers. It means looking at the best sellers and the worst sellers and the profit margins of each. It means maximizing the balance between sales numbers and margins. You may have to make some tough choices. There may be a product that you love and are proud of, but it is not selling well. If there isn't a solid business justification for keeping it, you may have to let that product go.

Inventory is a necessary expense, and you want to make sure those dollars are not being wasted on products that aren't helping your bottom line.

Marcus Lemonis, CEO of Camping World and star of the CNBC show *The Profit* is a big believer in having the right product mix. On his television show, he mentors struggling business owners, and product selection is a topic that frequently comes up. One of the best examples of him helping a business owner analyze their products is in Episode 10 of Season 3: "Bentley's Corner Barkery." The struggling business is a boutique pet store that has very specific standards for the types of food, treats, and toys they sell.

When Marcus first starts taking a look at their products, he notices that the price points are high. Because they're exclusively selling premium food that meets specific manufacturing and nutrition standards, the prices make sense, but when compared to a larger pet store chain like PetSmart, the prices at Bentley's seem outrageous. Concerned that this could be keeping some customers from shopping at Bentley's, Marcus suggests that they bring in a few less-expensive dog food brands (provided that they meet the owner's quality standards) in order to widen their customer base.

At first, the owners are resistant to the change because they're worried about diluting their brand. They are proud of their reputation as a high-end, quality brand, and they don't mind the fact that their target customer fits a narrow profile. Marcus's point, however, is that the business is struggling, and that more customers will lead to more sales, which will lead to more money for the business. To offset their concerns about brand dilution, he also brings in some premium treats and chew toys, which have higher price points and much higher margins than any of the food options.

The result in the end is that their core customers barely notice the change. They notice that the store looks cleaner and more streamlined because of some major merchandising changes, but they don't think much of the new food options. They continue buying the food brands they were buying before. The real success is that new people start coming into the store, and they are thrilled to see some high-quality, nutritious pet foods being offered at a reasonable price. They're happy with their experiences in the store and with the owners, and they're now loyal customers of Bentley's.

It can be hard to shake up your inventory, especially if you're attached to any of your products or if the product selection itself is attached to your values or your identity as a brand. Still, you have to look at the data. Make smart business decisions so that your products are moving your business in the right direction rather than holding it back. It may take you a few months of being open and analyzing your sales before you can tell if anything in your inventory needs to change, but you need to be thinking about it and looking at the numbers from day one.

The same concept holds true for service-oriented businesses. If there are services on your menu that require special equipment or significant labor hours, it's wise to take note of how often those specific services sell. You may find that they are not worth the cost in order to stay competitive in your industry, or that they have high enough margins that the costs are justified. The point is that it's important to know. You need to know what customers are responding to, what will keep them coming in the door, and what will have them recommending your business to their friends.

Pricing

It will take a little bit of time to figure out whether your pricing model is working or not, but start paying close attention to it from the very beginning. If you've been following our advice so far, you probably did a lot of market research on pricing before you launched, but we know things don't always go exactly as planned. Even the most well researched pricing models need to be adjusted sometimes.

In order to determine whether or not your pricing structure is working, you need to pay attention to what's happening in your own business, and you need to pay attention to your competition. Markets change, and so do customers. The absolute best thing you can do to make sure your prices are on par with the market is to stay up to date with news in your industry.

Have you heard complaints from customers about your prices? If so, you need to understand why. It could be that you're missing your target market and getting the wrong customers in the door in the first place. It could also be that your competitors are offering similar services for lower prices. Once you have a handle on what's happening, you can figure out if an adjustment needs to be made. It could be that you've misunderstood the market, and you now need to become more competitive with the other businesses in your industry. It could also be that you simply need to do a better job of offering customers more value for the prices you're charging.

Customer complaints are not an automatic indicator that you need to lower prices. They are an indicator, however, that you need to listen to feedback and do some research in order to figure out where the complaints are really coming from.

Changes in production costs are another thing that can force you to re-think your pricing structure. If they've gone up, talk to other business owners in your industry. Are they seeing the same thing? Is there a worldwide shortage of a particular material that's causing costs everywhere to go up? Or is the issue isolated to your business? If what's happening with production costs seems to be widespread in the industry, it may be time to raise prices in order to stay competitive and keep profits up. On the other hand, if it's just your vendors who have raised their prices, it's worth having a conversation with them to see if you can negotiate a better deal, or even switch vendors if you have to.

Pricing can be tricky, and it's normal to need to make an adjustment or two over time. Just be careful of making too many adjustments too quickly. Customers become confused, and quite frankly, scared, when they see prices changing. They expect consistency and will have a difficult time being loyal if prices often change without warning.

Another potential pitfall to watch out for is discounting. Discounts can be tempting, because they bring customers in the door. During those first few months, when you're desperate for any customers at all, it's a natural first instinct to want to offer promotional pricing and deep discounts. Do this at your own risk. Any time you put a price on a product or service, you're communicating to the customer what you think that product or service is worth. If you low-ball that price on purpose, you're training your customer to either expect low prices from you in the future, or to expect your product or service to have a lesser value.

Think about your own behavior as a consumer. When you get an email from a company offering a big 45% off sale, do you jump on it right away? Why or why not? If it's the first time they've ever put anything on sale, you might go for it, thinking that this is your chance to buy something that was previously out of your price range. But what if they run sales all the time? Why jump in when there's a 45% off sale when you know they're going to offer another discount (and maybe a bigger one!) in a week or two?

Discounts are not all good or all bad. They can be effective if used wisely and sparingly. The important thing to keep in mind is that they will affect the way customers see you and your business. Think about the potential effects before taking hasty action. If you're itching to get customers in the door, there are plenty of ways to do that without putting out random discounts.

Customer Data

Knowing who your customers are, where they're coming from, and some basic information about their attitudes and behaviors is extremely important in tailoring your business going forward. If you've done your homework in defining your target audience and reaching out to them accordingly, hopefully many of your early customers are right within that range. That's evidence that your marketing efforts are reaching the right people, and it means your business appeals to the people you expected it to.

It's not always so simple. Sometimes, especially when the business first opens, you'll get some customer traffic that seems random. This happens in retail locations when a curious passersby walks in. They may come in without any intention of making a purchase, but then change their mind if they like what they see. Random foot traffic is never a guarantee, but if you're lucky enough to have it, talk to those people! Find out what brought them in. Find out where they come from. Even if the conversation doesn't lead to an immediate sale, you may gather important information that can help your future marketing plans.

If you don't have a retail location, you're not going be seeing walk-in traffic, but you still may end up getting calls from people you would not have expected to become customers. If you've been doing any SEO or digital marketing, people will start to find you by doing keyword searches, and they're not always the people you're trying to reach. Again, always find out how people found you. Sometimes people outside your target range end up becoming great customers, and you may decide to tweak your marketing so that you're reaching a larger number of similar people.

On the flip side, if you're getting calls from a lot of people who never end up becoming customers, it's worth taking a look at your branding and messaging to make sure you're being very clear about what your company does. It's okay for leads to not pan out, but you don't want to be habitually wasting your time, either.

Another layer of analyzing customer data is looking at who is buying what. Are men buying more of a certain product than women? Are people in their 20's latching onto particular products or services that aren't selling as well with an older crowd? What kinds of people are spending the most money with you? When you break down sales and look for patterns within your customers, you can make wise decisions about what you are selling and how you are selling it. You may need to adjust your products or services so that you're appealing to a wider base, like Bentley's Corner Barkley did, or you may find that your best option is to maximize your sales to the people you have. In other words, if the majority of your sales are to women between the ages of 35-45, make sure most of your products are tailored to that demographic.

Some business owners are afraid to gather customer data because they worry that it's intrusive. We're not saying that you need to be pushy or ask for a bunch of private information and make customers feel uncomfortable, but you should be gathering basic statistics that will help you grow your business and appeal to the right people. Most customers these days are accustomed to providing information to businesses and won't think anything of being asked a few questions. Plus, if your business requires you to build close relationships with your customers, you'll get a lot of this information through casual conversation anyway.

Solicit Feedback

One great way to find out how your business is doing and what you can do to do better is to talk to your customers. You're too close to the inner workings of the business to be able to see exactly what customers see. You need to hear from them to know for sure what their experiences are like. This is different than asking for reviews or testimonials. This is not asking them to share their opinions with the world; this is asking them to analyze your business critically and to give you specific feedback on what would improve the customer experience.

After being in business for a few months, especially if you've had some success, it's tempting to assume that if there were anything customers didn't like about your business, they'd have told you. The truth is, people rarely give unsolicited feedback. Even the types of people who give negative reviews online are much less likely to call your business and deliver that feedback personally. Most people avoid confrontation in that way.

The people who will likely feel the most comfortable being blunt and honest with you are people with whom you've built a relationship. If you're in a service business, maybe you have a client who you've been working with over a period of weeks or a few months. If you have a retail location, maybe you've noticed a few regulars. Pull them aside for a few minutes or send them an email, and ask for whatever feedback they're willing to give.

Most customers will consider this an honor. They'll be glad that you value them enough to ask for their opinions, and they'll likely be motivated to put some thought into it. Customers don't always have your business front of mind, so they may not realize that something could be better or more efficient until they are prompted to think about it. If you have specific questions for them, that's even more helpful and will probably give you more useful feedback, but a general ask is better than no ask at all.

When you get some responses, you need to handle them wisely. First and foremost, thank anyone who provided you with feedback and let them know that you're taking it seriously. People need to know they've been heard, especially when they've taken the time to think about your business and help you out. This is easy and obvious if you're having an in-person conversation, but if someone emails you feedback, do not forget to respond!

Next, evaluate all the feedback you've received, and don't just gloss over it. Really look at it with a critical eye. Are there patterns in what people are saying? Is there something that people seem to be dancing around and not saying directly? What would happen if you implemented some of the suggestions? If what you're hearing from customers is reasonable and realistic, it's smart to listen and make some changes.

Asking for direct feedback helps you as a business owner, and it makes your customers feel valuable. Once you've done it one time, your customers will be more likely to offer you unsolicited feedback in the future. Even if you work in a business where customer interactions are short, having open communication with customers is always a good thing. It will strengthen your business, and your customers will become fiercely loyal.

Finally, solicit feedback from a friend or loved one who will not be afraid to be honest with you. They probably watched you as you went through all of the stages of launching your business, and they have a unique perspective. They're too close to the business to see it the way your customers do, but they have a sense of objectivity you don't have.

In the first few weeks after you launch your business, have this friend or loved one observe you as you interact with customers. Whether they watch you interact with a person, or whether they observe you while you're on the phone, they will be able to provide you with feedback you wouldn't otherwise get. They know you personally, so they'll immediately know if you're acting genuinely or not, and they'll also be able to tell you if any of your habits or less desirable qualities are showing through. For example, some people start to talk fast and raise their voice when they start to get really excited or passionate about a topic. Over the phone, that could come across as anger or as being overbearing.

This isn't to say that you need to change your personality to try and please every customer, but you do need to be aware of your behaviors so that you can understand how people perceive you. To have one person not click with you is fine, but if multiple customers are being turned off because of how you come across, that could be a problem. Ultimately, you're the one who gets to decide whether or not you change anything in how you communicate with customers, but it's important to at least be aware.

Asking for feedback can be scary. You never know what people are going to say, and being criticized is not fun. It's worth doing, though. You can fix anything you know about, and it is far better to start getting out in front of potential issues rather than to have them come back and bite you later.

╫ Matt: One thing I started analyzing is how long it was taking each client to pay. I was noticing that some clients were paying slower and slower, and that seemed odd to me. I wanted to understand what was going on. I would ask clients what was taking so long, and they all said basically the same thing. They were used to paying for things with credit cards, and Modmacro only took checks. It was an inconvenience, and it slowed people down.

The thing is, no one was going to volunteer that information. They weren't thinking, "I should tell Matt to start taking credit cards," because it wasn't on their mind all the time. They only thought about it when it came time to write a check. I had to be paying attention to notice the pattern in the first place, and then to ask clients directly about it. After hearing multiple people tell me how much easier it would be to pay by card, I made it happen. Now, people are paying about ten times faster than they were.

In addition to taking credit cards, we also discovered that customers preferred to have an annual contract with monthly automatic payments rather than paying for each month separately. It streamlined everything and made it hassle-free for everyone. I didn't think customers would want that kind of commitment, so I didn't set the business up that way in the beginning. I had to ask for feedback about it, and when I realized I could make my customers' lives easier, I did it. People love things that are hassle-free, and if you can remove inconveniences for your customers, they'll gravitate towards you that much more.

✚ Jessica: For us at Maven, we're still trying to wrap our heads around how people are finding us and what kinds of things they are looking for. We did so much research and planning around who our target customer would be, and while we're getting calls from those people, we're also getting calls from people who fall pretty far outside what we expected. This isn't a bad thing at all; we've been getting creative and coming up with solutions to help people with things we didn't initially plan on doing.

We're happy to stretch ourselves and pick up new skills in order to take care of people. It's exciting and interesting, and since the publishing world is always changing, we're glad to have the opportunity to get involved with bigger aspects of the business that we didn't originally intend on get into. At the same time, we're wondering how some of these people are finding us and what we're saying in our messaging that is bringing these types of clients in.

It's a good "problem" to have. No one is complaining. We're just surprised by it, and it's an indicator that we need to pay attention and gather as much data as possible. We need to understand how people are seeing our company from the outside, and we may ultimately need to make some changes to make our messaging more precise. We are still a young company, and we have a lot to learn about who our customers are and what they want.

Who Are You Building Relationships With?

ANY EXPERIENCED BUSINESS owner will tell you that the success or failure of a business often depends on relationships. That could mean relationships with customers, or it could mean relationships with partners, vendors, investors, your city, and even your competitors. Even though your business is still young, it's never too early to start building relationships and making sure you get off on the right foot with people who will help you succeed.

Customers

No matter what kind of business you're running, maintaining a steady flow of new and repeat customers is the key to keeping it going. New customers will come as a result of effective marketing and word-of-mouth, and repeat customers will come as a result of doing great work with each and every one of your customers.

This will look different, depending on the type of business you have. For example, if you own a food truck, you don't need to get to know each of your customers' life stories, but you do need to treat them well if you want them to come back. On the other hand, if you're a window installer, you have to meet customers in their homes. This means you have to get to know them well enough to build trust, or else they will be hesitant to allow your crew in the door to get the job done.

You may find that this evolves over time. After being open for a while and completing a number of jobs, you may discover that you want to invest more time in building customer relationships. Connecting with your customers is never a bad thing. Even in restaurants, where customers quickly shuffle in and out, it pays off to notice people who come back again and again and to get to know them.

Vendors

If your business requires that you to work with suppliers and manufacturers, you need to invest heavily in those relationships. You need to work closely with them to maintain quality control, and the better your relationship, the more leverage you'll have if you need to negotiate price or if you need to have a conversation about deadlines or expectations.

Problems with vendors can quickly wreck a business. Anyone who is partnering with you on the supply end needs to understand your business and its mission, and they need to adhere to your standards. If you're having trouble working with a vendor for whatever reason, it may be time to make a change. In the beginning, it makes sense to want to give someone a fair chance, but remember how fragile your reputation is when you first launch. If you start off with vendor problems, and they can't be remedied quickly by working on the relationship, find someone else to work with before it negatively impacts your customers.

Partners, Co-Workers, and Employees

Launching a business is a crazy time, and it can get stressful. It seems like no matter how well you plan, something always turns out differently than you expected. When things get chaotic, tensions run high, and if you don't already have great relationships with the people you're working with, it's that much worse. With all the external stresses of the first few weeks and months after launch, it's important to make sure everything internally is running as smoothly as possible. Customers can feel it when something negative is going on behind the scenes, so be sure to take care of your people, no matter how crazy it gets.

As time goes on, and as you become a more experienced business owner, you're going to go through ups and downs. You'll face new challenges all the time, and the benefit of working with others is that you'll have multiple minds to work through those challenges. The best way to make sure you all stay focused on the mission at hand is to start off by building a strong company culture. Defining your company culture right from the start makes it easy to manage expectations and resolve conflict when it arises.

Just like your products, your facility, and your equipment, your people are assets. Always be investing in those relationships, and you'll have a much easier time weathering any storm that comes at your business.

Attorneys, Accountants, and Other Professionals

Throughout this entire book, we've talked about the importance of working with professionals for certain tasks. We've discussed how things like accounting and legal issues are better left to the people who do those things for a living. This not only ensures that they have a better chance of being done correctly, but it also allows you to spend your time focusing on your business.

If you've been following our advice so far, then you already have relationships with some professionals. Continue to build those relationships. Stay in touch, even when you don't urgently need them. The more they know about you and your business, the more they'll be able to help you, not to mention the fact that they'll be more likely to make your needs a priority when you do call with a request. Some business owners go an entire year without keeping in touch with their accountant, and then when they need their books reconciled at the end of the year, the accountant has to spend a bunch of time re-familiarizing themselves with the company.

You don't have to be annoying, nor do you have to be emailing or calling people all the time, but don't be a stranger. Feel free to reach out with questions here and there. Share successes. Just keep the relationships going.

City Officials and Property Owners

This may not apply to everyone, but if you have a business that requires getting permits or setting up shop in different places on different days, this is important. Bureaucracy can be difficult, and the less of it you have to deal with, the better. You'll be able to cut through it much more easily if you have relationships with people in the right organizations and offices.

Again, think about a food truck business. A food truck owner needs to have city or county permits to operate, as well as certifications from the health department. Food trucks also usually change locations from day to day, often parking on other businesses' properties. In order to accomplish all of these things, it helps to build relationships. The first time you interact with the various officials you need to talk to, make sure you are cordial and patient, and then from there, do your best to follow regulations and be accommodating. It's amazing how much more likely they will be willing to help you in the future if they remember you as someone who is easy to work with.

At the end of the day, you need to look at your business and prioritize how you build relationships. All of these relationships are important, but certain ones will be more important than others at the beginning. Build good relationships from the start, and never stop working on them. When you stop actively working on relationships, you start to take people for granted, and that can easily slide into taking advantage of people, even if you're not intending to. Good relationships will help you propel your business forward, but broken relationships can stop you in your tracks.

╫ Matt: For my business, it's important that I maintain healthy relationships with clients. To keep those relationships strong, I try to measure people's happiness. It's not an exact science, but once I get to know people, I can generally tell at the end of a conversation how happy they are. For example, sometimes clients will call about some new marketing technique they heard about and ask if it would be good for them. Even though I'm the marketing expert, and even if I give them a really well-articulated and thought-out answer as to why their suggestion isn't a good idea for their business, they're not happy with hearing "no." They thought they had a good idea, and they wanted me to support it.

I don't want to leave conversations with a client who's unhappy. It may be a while before we talk again, and if the last thing they remember was that I shot down their idea, that could wear away at our relationship. I have to figure out what to do in real time. I'll do my best to come up with an alternative solution that incorporates pieces of their idea, just so they know I heard them, and so they know I wasn't trying to be insulting. I'm usually able to smooth things over and leave the conversation in a good place.

The other thing I've been noticing lately is that people I'm meeting for the first time can hear how passionate I am about my business. They'll tell me, "Man, you're really into this stuff!" And it's true. I am genuinely passionate about helping them grow their business through digital marketing. It's not something that I'm faking to get the right perception. I guess I hadn't thought about the fact that there are plenty of marketing professionals out there who have gotten tired and complacent. That's not a good way to build and keep relationships. People want to work with people who care about what they're doing.

╫ Jessica: Collaborating on creating a book is such a personal process. Without a strong relationship with a client, we can't get anything done. Like Matt has said, keeping people happy is paramount. It doesn't mean being a pushover and letting clients take advantage of me. It just means that they need to feel like this process is as much theirs as it is Maven's. It means making adjustments to the process when needed and personalizing each project. That sounds like a big investment, and it is, but the payoff is huge. People trust us, and they find joy in the process of creating something together.

The other relationship we are always aware of is our relationship to the publishing industry as a whole. With how much the industry has changed in the digital age, companies are popping up all the time and trying to capitalize on the low barriers to entry. Frankly, a lot of them are trying to make some quick money and disappear. It's frustrating for companies like ours, because we are truly passionate about what we do, and we intend to be around for a very, very long time. It's important that the industry categorizes us as one of the "good guys."

Forging relationships with established companies and with prominent players in the industry is important to us. We want people to know who we are and to understand what we're doing. There's a lot of competition in publishing, but there's a lot of cooperation, also. The companies who cooperate with each other are the ones who make it, and that's who we want to be.

What's Going On Internally?

ONCE YOU'VE LAUNCHED your business, you have about a thousand balls in the air. While you're evaluating the success of your business, your inventory selection, your customer data, and your relationships with various people related to your business, you may forget to look at your own internal processes. If you're just scrambling to keep everything going from day to day (managing the chaos, rather than controlling it) it's important to slow down and look at what's going on inside the business.

Like we discussed earlier in this chapter, your first priority needs to be to take care of your people. If you have partners, co-workers, or employees, talk to them and solicit feedback. Make sure they're getting what they need from you, and work to resolve any conflicts as quickly as you can. Set expectations, hold everyone accountable (including yourself), and let people know that they're valued.

Next, look at your processes. When you start your own company, you're not handed a book of corporate Standard Operating Procedures (SOPs) to follow; you have to invent them yourself. You'll have your own way of doing things, and it's wise to make it as simple, streamlined, and repeatable as possible.

Those of you who are working alone or with only one or two people may not think this is important. You probably all know how to do your jobs, and you don't need to have a big discussion about it. That's fair enough. But what happens if your company grows? What if you need to hire someone new? Many business owners are a little caught off guard when this happens, and they say things like, "If only I had another 'me' to help get things done around here." It would be convenient to have another "you" with your brain and your experience, but the reality is that if you hire someone, they will have their own brain, and you will have to teach them things.

It's not natural for most people to document what they're doing as they're doing it. After all, if you have a process committed to memory, why spend time writing it down? The reason to write it down is so that you can easily pass that knowledge on to someone else.

To help you start thinking about this, here's an exercise:

Fast forward to a year from now. Imagine that your business is successful and that you're completely overwhelmed with customers, jobs, and work. You can no longer handle it on your own, and you need to bring someone in to help you out. That could be an assistant for yourself, or it could be someone to duplicate one of the positions you already have (i.e. another programmer). The person you hire will probably have some experience in your industry, but they will still need to learn the way you do things at your company.

What does this person need to know? What processes will they be responsible for? What tasks will be handed to this person, and how do you do them? You've probably done every task in your business so many times you can do them in your sleep, so you may actually have to really slow down and think about how to do things step-by-step. You may even have to repeat the task solely for the purpose of recording the steps.

It seems like extra work, we know. Trust us, this will help you immensely down the line. Not only will you save yourself the stress and frustration of trying to teach someone a task without following a step-by-step outline, but you will also become more efficient at the task yours

You may not be able to do this with every single task, and that's okay. Some tasks will be too complex or too situational to come up with a repeatable SOP. Start with the simple tasks that you need to do often, and go from there. Don't grind your business to a halt to create an encyclopedia of SOPs, but spend a little time on it each week, and by the time you need to hire that extra person, you'll have excellent training guidelines for them. You'll be relieved, and they will thank you for it, too.

For those of you who are working alone and have no desire to grow beyond that, maybe SOPs are not for you. Not everyone needs them. Some people like to have them for themselves for tasks that they don't do often and therefore forget. Some people also find that written SOPs help them do tasks more quickly. These are personal preferences, and you can decide what works for you.

Our suggestion is always: if something isn't working, change it. If you're forgetting how to do certain things, try writing the process down so you can reference it the next time you have to do it. Likewise, if you spent time writing down SOPs, and you never, ever reference them; maybe don't spend time on that again. If your company is just you and it always will be, you have total freedom to cater to your own personal preference.

✠ Matt: At the end of last year, my assistant and I met with an accountant for the first time. She walked us through everything we needed to do to close out our books at the end of each year before bringing them to her so that we'd be prepared for the following year. While it was nice of her to do it for us the one time, I didn't want to forget the process and have to re-learn it again in 11 months. So when we got back to the office, I told my assistant that we needed to run through the process one more time.

I had her document every step of the process. It was extra work to have to do it again, and even more extra work to write it all down, but I wanted to be sure it would always be done correctly. Plus, what if my assistant were busy with something else at the end of the year and a different person had to close out the books? Would either one of us have time to try and recall everything from memory and train someone? Probably not. Now, we can hand the list off, and we can have confidence that all steps will be completed.

Not all people think in an operational way. It takes discipline to slow down and put that kind of time investment in up front. If this is not your natural tendency, my best advice is to start training yourself to do it anyway. You never know what's going to happen in the future, and if you or a different member of your team is suddenly gone, will someone else be able to easily step in and pick up the tasks?

╫ Jessica: For those of you in creative fields, it's tempting to say, "Well nothing about what I do is linear or repeatable. It's always different." And that may be true in your line of work. Not much about writing is linear, and every writer has a unique process that works for them. Still, you own a business. Many business owner tasks are very linear, and if most of your time is focused on the creative aspect of your work, then you probably don't practice the business owner stuff as often. Anything that isn't practiced often is prone to being forgotten.

What I'm saying is do yourself a favor, and write down the things that can be written down. For us, that includes bookkeeping and accounting tasks. It includes formulas and spreadsheets for tracking sales. It includes the step-by-step instructions for properly uploading and cataloguing files with the various online platforms like Amazon and iBooks. Every business has some tasks that are virtually the same every time. Don't waste time re-learning how to do those tasks each time you do them. Make a list, and follow it.

Now What?

You've LAUNCHED YOUR business, and you're well on your way to success. Things will probably feel busy and chaotic for a while. It can take months and even years before you truly feel comfortable as a brand new business owner. And of course, just when you start to feel like you know what you're doing, something in the market will shift, or you'll be offered a huge opportunity that you didn't expect, and you'll feel busy and chaotic again.

As long as you own your business, you'll always be learning. If you're following our advice and evaluating every piece of your business as you grow and develop, you'll constantly be finding new ways to do things. You'll probably have a million ideas throughout your time as an entrepreneur, some of which will be great, and some of which will be terrible. You'll try things, you'll make mistakes, you'll learn, and you'll get better. Some of you will even fail. Many of the world's most successful entrepreneurs have had at least one failed business; what's made them great is the fact that they got right back up again and applied what they learned to a brand new venture.

So, what now?

Run your business. Set goals and surpass them. Aim to avoid failure, but don't be afraid of it, either. Seek out other business owners both inside and outside of your industry and learn everything you can from them. When you get overwhelmed, take a small step. Focus on the one thing in front of you. Just always keep moving.

We hope this advice has helped you as you've gone from idea to launch, and we hope you revisit pieces of this book as needed. Much of the advice can be as applicable to a 10-year-old business as it is to a 10-day-old business.

Good luck, and we hope each day as an entrepreneur is as exciting for you as it has been for us.

Note to Readers

Thank you for taking the time to read this book. We hope you found it to be inspiring, and we hope it has helped you get closer to your goal of launching your own business. We would greatly appreciate your feedback in the form of an honest review on Amazon or on whichever site you bought the book.

For more compelling content and insightful interviews geared towards small business owners and entrepreneurs check out Modmacro's digital publication, *Businessing Magazine.*

http://businessingmag.com

If you'd like to contact either of us personally or find out more about our companies, we would love to hear from you!

To contact Matt:
Email: matt@modmacro.com
LinkedIn: www.linkedin.com/in/Modmacro
Google+: plus.google.com/+MattSmithModmacro
www.modmacro.com

To contact Jessica:
Email: jdawson@maven-books.com
LinkedIn: www.linkedin.com/in/JessicaTDawson1
Google+: plus.google.com/+Maven-Books
www.maven-books.com

About the Authors

Matt Smith is the Founder and CEO of Modmacro, an award-winning digital marketing firm in Southern California. Author of Kill the Noise, a book about streamlining your business, Matt's approach challenges established digital marketing tactics and thinking.

An engineer by education, Matt has focused more than a decade on software development and small business marketing. Founding Modmacro in 2010, his role involves directing the company while remaining intimately involved in client projects on a daily basis.

Jessica Dawson is the CEO and Co-founder of Maven Publishing USA, a boutique publishing house of non-fiction that focuses on turning entrepreneurs, business owners, and professionals into published authors. Every business has a story, but few business owners have the time to devote to learning the fine details of writing and publishing. Jessica and her team collaborate with busy professionals to create books that become powerful marketing assets and help to position the authors as experts in their fields.

About Modmacro

An award-winning web design and marketing firm, Modmacro partners with select small businesses to strategically grow their companies. Their integrated marketing approach is based on a healthy mix of original creativity (design), visual appeal (branding), authentic story sharing (PR), driving targeted traffic (SEO), original content creation, user experience design considerations (UX), and practical data insights (analytics).

The company delivers tailor-made marketing solutions whose results illustrate clear value to profit-minded decision makers. Through a simple, proven process, Modmacro's approach often challenges established thinking and reboots the status quo. They invest in educating clients with the goal of developing lasting, partnership-level relationships that foster candid, productive dialogue.

About Maven Publishing

Maven Publishing is a boutique writing, editing, and publishing house of non-fiction, making published authors of entrepreneurs, business people, and professionals, who are then superiorly branded and positioned by their book(s).

From financial advisers to CEOs to nutritionists to relationship experts, the team at Maven has worked with all types of busy professionals who should have books but who don't have the time to learn the fine details of writing and publishing. Maven works with clients at any stage of the book creation process and makes sure they get to the finish line.

www.ingramcontent.com/pod-product-compliance
Lightning Source LLC
Chambersburg PA
CBHW032007190326
41520CB00007B/392